ARCTIC LANDS

ARCTIC LANDS

VIKING LANDS

Baltic Sea

Europe

ROME

Black Sea

ANCIENT GREECE

Caspian Sea

Mediterranean Sea

Asia

JAPAN

Sea of Japan

ANCIENT EGYPT

MESOPOTAMIA

CHINA

Persian Gulf

ANCIENT INDIA

Red Sea

Arabian Sea

Bay of Bengal

South China Sea

Africa

Indian Ocean

Australia

Cape of Good Hope

TRAVEL, CONQUEST & WARFARE

through the ages

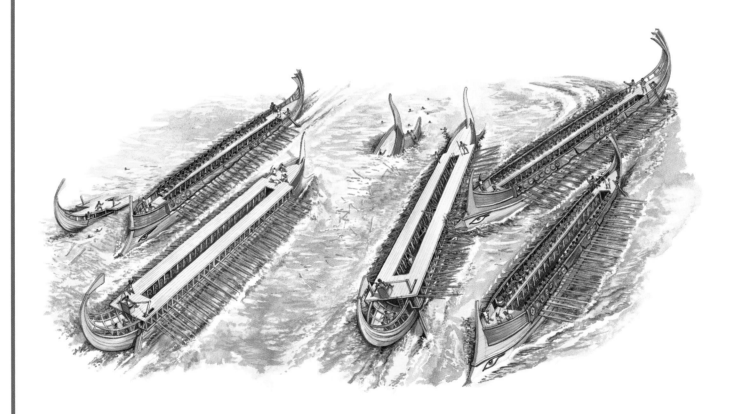

Series Editor Dr John Haywood

LORENZ BOOKS

First published by Lorenz Books in 2001

© Anness Publishing Limited 2001

Lorenz Books is an imprint of Anness Publishing Limited,
Hermes House, 88–89 Blackfriars Road, London SE1 8HA

www.lorenzbooks.com

This edition distributed in Canada by Raincoast Books, 9050
Shaughnessy Street, Vancouver, British Columbia,
V6P 6E5

A CIP catalogue record for this book is available from the
British Library.

Publisher Joanna Lorenz
Manager, Children's Books and Contributing Editor Gilly
Cameron Cooper
Project Editor Rasha Elsaeed
Assistant Editor Sarah Uttridge
Editorial Reader Joy Wotton
Authors Daud Ali, Jen Green, Charlotte Hurdman, Fiona
Macdonald, Lorna Oakes, Philip Steele, Michael Stotter,
Richard Tames
Consultants Nick Allen, Cherry Alexander, Clara Bezanilla,
Felicity Cobbing, Penny Dransart, Jenny Hall, Dr John
Haywood, Dr Robin Holgate, Michael Johnson, Lloyd Laing,
Jessie Lim, Heidi Potter, Louise Schofield, Leslie Webster,
Designers Simon Borrough, Matthew Cook, John Jamieson,
Joyce Mason, Caroline Reeves, Margaret Sadler, Alison Walker,
Stuart Watkinson at Ideas Into Print, Sarah Williams
Special Photography John Freeman
Stylists Konika Shakar, Thomasina Smith, Melanie Williams

Previously published as part of the *Step Into* series in 14
separate volumes:
*Ancient Egypt, Ancient Greece, Ancient India, Ancient Japan,
Arctic World, Aztec & Maya Worlds, Celtic World, Chinese
Empire, Inca World, Mesopotamia, North American Indians,
Roman Empire, Viking World, The Stone Age.*

PICTURE CREDITS
b=bottom, t=top, c=centre, l=left, r=right

AKG: 16br, 27c, 42tl, 44tr, 49t, 56b, 58bl, 59t, 51b, 60tl,
61tr; Lesley and Roy Adkins: 37tl; B and C Alexander: 9tl,
23tl, 23cr; The Ancient Art and Architecture Collection
Ltd:10l, 11r, 14tl, 16br, 31b, 33tl, 34tr, 36tr, 38tl, 41tr, 45tl;
Japan Archive: 31tr, 32tl; Bildarchiv Preussischer Kulturbesitz
– 26tl, 26cl; The Bridgeman Art Library: 17tr, 17bl, 17br,
29br, 46b, 47tr, 47cl, 55bl; The British Museum: 39b; Bruce
Coleman: 25bl; Bulloz: 26cr; Christies: 30bl, 30br, 31tl, 33bl;
Corbis-Bettman: 48b, 48tl, 49bl, 58br, 60bl, 61bl; Corbis:
23bl, 18bl, 49b, 58tl; Sue Cunningham Photographic: 54tr,
56cr; James Davis: 21c; C.M Dixon: 8tl, 15cl, 34cl, 35tr, 37tr,
37b, 38l, 39tr, 43tl, 43tr, 44br, 46tr, 51c, 61tl; E.T Archive
(Art Archive): 12bl, 15cl, 17tr, 28tl, 28cr, 29t, 25r, 28tl, 28br,
29tr, 45tr, 45bl, 52br, 54tl, 56tl; Planet Earth pictures: 22bl;
Mary Evans Picture Library: 21t, 23tr, 25tl, 35cl, 36br, 38r,
52tl, 57b; Fine Art Photographic Library: 40c; Werner Forman
Archive: 9c, 13tr, 19cl, 43bl, 43c, 47tl, 55cl; Fortean Picture
Library: 8r; Idemitsu Museum of Arts: 33cl; Images Colour
Library: 19tr; Robert Harding: 19tr, 20tl, 21t; Michael
Holford: 18tl, 19t, 27t, 30tl, 32br, 36bl, 45br, 53; Radio Times
Hulton Picture Library: 10r, 11r; Jenny Laing: 41tl, 41bl;
MacQuitty Collection: 12tl, 13cl, 13br; Peter Newark's
Pictures: 59tr; Oxford Scientific Films: 22tl; Mick Sharp: 40tl,
47br; Skyscan: 41br; South American Picture Library: 50t, 53,
54c, 55t, 56tl, 57tr; Visual Arts Library: 13tl, 14cl, 24c, 51t,
52bl; Zefa: 10r, 11l

10 9 8 7 6 5 4 3 2 1

CONTENTS

KEY
Look out for the border patterns used throughout this book.
They will help you to identify each culture.

The Stone Age	Roman Empire
Mesopotamia	The Celts
Ancient Egypt	The Vikings
India	North American Indians
China	The Arctic
Japan	Aztec & Maya
Ancient Greece	Inca Empire

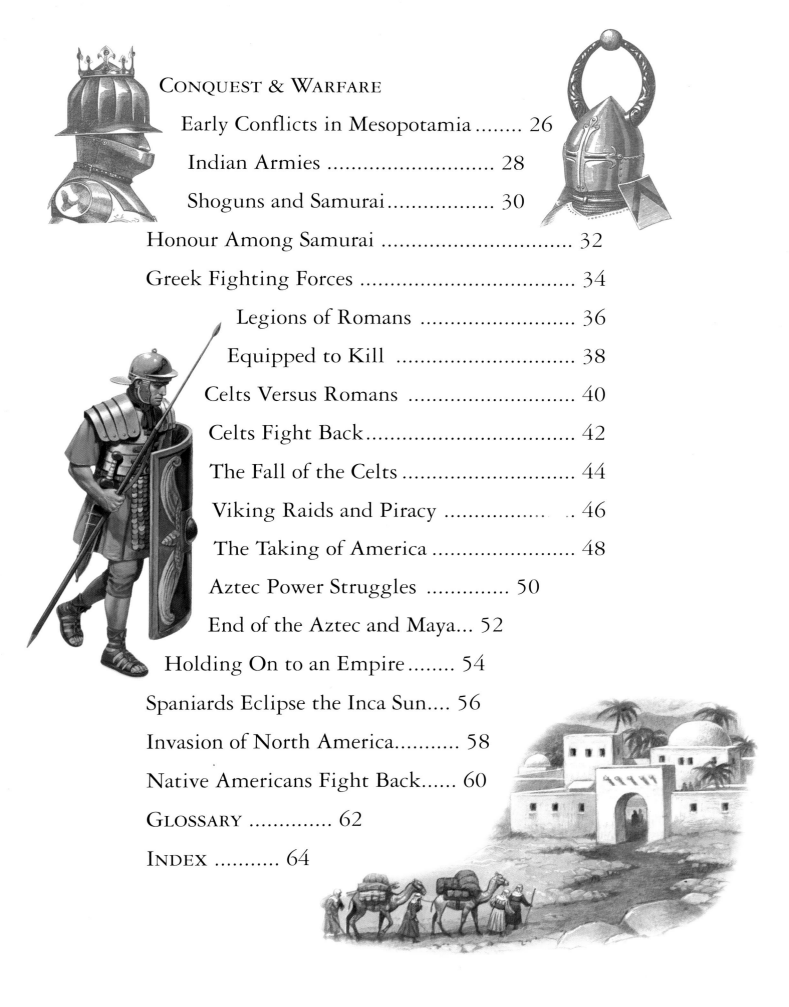

CONQUEST & WARFARE

Breaking New Frontiers

Early humans were always on the move, searching for wild animals and plants for food. They had to walk everywhere. They had not learned how to tame such animals as wild oxen or asses to carry them. But then, the hunter-gatherers did not feel the need to develop new methods of transport, because they did not have much to carry around.

Gradually, some humans learned how to cultivate wild grasses into reliable crops. They built permanent shelters in the fertile river valleys and farmed there. They wanted and needed to find out how to grow better food, and to store and transport it. Life was no longer the scrabble for survival that it had been for their earliest ancestors.

They had time to work out how to make improvements. New and better methods of transport and travel were used in peacetime and in war.

Populations increased in the fertile farmlands. People moved in search of new places to live, and with this, came the need to travel.

Early humans were always on the move, looking for food. They had not learned how to tame animals that could be ridden or used to pull vehicles.

The Polynesians roamed the ocean of the South Pacific seeking new islands to settle. Over 2,000 years ago they could navigate the seas successfully, and travel over vast expanses of empty ocean in sail-powered canoes.

TIMELINE 100,000–200BC

100,000 years ago. Nomadic bands of hunter-gatherers migrate north out of Africa into the Middle East in search of new hunting grounds.

50,000 years ago. The ancestors of the Aborigines become the earliest people to build boats or rafts when they sail from Asia to Australia.

Early humans used their upright stance to gather berries

10,000BC Humans have discovered every continent except ice-covered Antarctica.

8000BC Beginning of farming in the Middle East.

4500BC The first Mesopotamian sailing ships are built.

3800BC Metal weapons, made of bronze, come into use in the Middle East.

3500BC The first wheeled vehicles are made in Mesopotamia.

3000BC Age of the oldest surviving large ships, discovered buried in the desert in Egypt.

1500BC War chariots are used by the Assyrians and Egyptians to carry archers into battle.

bronze spearheads

100,000BC   **10,000BC**   **3500BC**   **1500BC**

As people travelled to lands already settled by others, they had to fight to win new territory. Both travel and war led to the spread of new inventions and ideas, and the incentive to create ever better transport and weapons.

Farming communities were producing more goods than they needed for themselves. Surplus produce could be transported to other regions and traded. With

Horsedrawn chariots could travel fast over the battlefield. The Hittites, who lived in a region that is now part of modern Turkey, were among the first to use horses in warfare. They made the chariot one of the most feared weapons of war around 1600 to 1200BC.

expansion and trade, came the need for faster, safer and more reliable methods of travel. Farmers tamed animals such as the horse and ox for carrying goods and people from place to place, and then realized that the animals could also pull ploughs to till the soil.

About 6,000 years ago, the Mesopotamians harnessed the wind by hoisting sails on their boats. Sailing in the open ocean is dangerous even in today's yachts. Imagine then what it must have been like for Phoenician traders, who, from about 850BC, were sailing from the eastern Mediterranean into the Atlantic Ocean.

Sometimes, people wanted to travel and conquer just because they were greedy. A successful farmer might fancy taking over someone else's land just to increase the size of his own farm and give him more wealth and power. A neighbouring tribe or region

Expert horsemen were at an advantage over footsoldiers. Persian soldiers had horses that were strong and nimble, and the rider could wield a weapon from a height.

Assyrian war chariot

1500BC The Saami in Arctic Europe invent skis for travelling over snow.

1000BC Iron weapons and tools come into widespread use in the Middle East and Europe.

800BC The Greeks begin to fight as hoplites (armoured infantry).

387BC The Celts sack Rome.

312BC The Romans start to build a road system throughout the Empire.

221BC Shi Huangdi founds the Chinese Empire.

Greek galley

1500BC   350BC   200BC

might have something another tribe wanted such as fertile soil, timber or metal. Conflict was an inevitable result. Celts and Vikings fought over cattle and land. Monarchs and emperors fought for control of whole countries.

Unfortunately it is often war that provides the spur to technological improvements. If you want to win a race or a battle, you make sure you have the best equipment. The warlike Hittites were among the first to ride horses into battle and use iron weapons. Their country in south-eastern Europe was landlocked, and they fought for control of ports and trade in the Mediterranean Sea. The Mesopotamians upgraded the solid-wheeled cart into an effective war chariot with spoked wheels.

Early Egyptian life centred on the River Nile, so the Egyptians were experts in making river boats. Later, they wanted to trade farther afield and built seagoing boats like this with huge sails.

Both trade and empire-building encouraged the spread and exchange of ideas and technology. The horse was introduced to North America by the Europeans in the 1500s and it completely transformed how North American Indians hunted, travelled and fought. Phoenician traders and Greek adventurers took their

In the Middle Ages, battles were fought on horseback. Christian and Saracen Muslims knights often clashed during the Crusades, a series of conflicts in the Middle East. The Europeans picked up some useful ideas on castle and weapon design from their foes.

TIMELINE 200BC–AD1900

191BC–AD43 The Romans conquer the Celts in northern Europe.

AD476 Fall of the Western Roman Empire. The Eastern Empire survives until 1453.

AD793 Viking pirates begin to attack Britain and Ireland.

AD800 The Chinese build their first large ships, called junks, with many masts and proper rudders.

Viking longship

AD969 Gunpowder is used in war for the first time, in China.

AD1000 The Viking Leif Eriksson becomes the first European to reach America.

1100 Samurai warriors become important in warfare in Japan.

Chinese fireworks

200BC   AD800   AD900   1300

shipbuilding expertise throughout the Mediterranean and beyond. The superb metalworking crafsmanship of the Saracen Muslims east of the Mediterranean, spread to northern Europe.

Roman galleys were used mostly for war. They had picked up the galley design from the Greeks. Oarpower allowed for manoeuvrability in close combat.

The geography of a country shapes the way in which its transport and war-waging develops. The Greeks were great seafarers partly because of their endless coastline, but also because there was a limited amount of fertile land in their rugged country. The Vikings, trapped in narrow coastal strips beneath the mountains of Scandinavia, built ships that crossed the Atlantic Ocean to America. They were also fearsome warriors. The Incas in South America had a major road network and wheeled toys, but no wheeled vehicles. As in the mountains of Japan, walking over steep, narrow tracks was faster and safer than wheeled transport.

As you turn these pages, you will see how different countries and cultures travelled and conquered – and developed transport and weapons.

The Spanish went to Mesoamerica greedy for Aztec gold. The Aztecs were fierce fighters but no match for the Spanish, on horseback, with their gunpowder and steel.

1492 Columbus 'discovers' America while searching for a route to China.

1521 The Spanish under Cortés conquer the Aztecs.

1526 The Mughals begin to take over India.

Christopher Columbus

1532 The Spanish under Francisco Pizarro conquer the Incas.

1607 The English begin to settle in Virginia in North America.

1776 The United States declares independence from Britain.

Francisco Pizzaro

1868 The Tokugawa Dynasty of shoguns comes to an end in Japan.

1890 The 'Battle' of Wounded Knee ends the Indian Wars in the United States. Native Indians are confined to reservations.

a Huron brave

1500   1800   1900

Stone Age People On the Move

THE EARLIEST MEANS of transport, apart from travelling on foot, was by boat. The first people to reach Australia, around 50,000BC, probably paddled log or bamboo rafts across the open ocean. Later Stone Age peoples made skin-covered coracles, kayaks (canoes) hollowed from tree trunks and boats made from reeds. Wooden sledges or *travois* (triangular platforms of poles lashed together) were dragged to carry goods and people overland. People pushed logs to act as rollers beneath very heavy objects such as rocks. The taming of horses, donkeys, camels and oxen revolutionized land transport. The first roads and causeways in Europe were built around the same time. By about 3500BC, the wheel had been invented in Egypt and Mesopotamia.

HORSE'S HEAD
This rock engraving of a horse's head comes from a cave in France. Some experts think that horses may have been tamed as early as 12,000BC. There are carvings that appear to show bridles around the heads of horses, although these could indicate manes.

CORACLE
A man fishes from a coracle, one of the oldest boat designs. Made of animal hide stretched over a wooden frame, the coracle may have been used since about 7600BC.

MAKE A MODEL CANOE
You will need: card, pencil, ruler, scissors, pva glue, glue brush, masking tape, self-drying clay, double-sided sticky tape, chamois leather, pair of compasses, thread, needle.

canoe top
———20cm———
canoe top
—10cm –
canoe base
———20cm———
canoe base
—10cm—

1 Cut card to the size of the templates shown on the left. Remember to cut semicircles from the long edge of both top pieces.

2 Glue the bases together and the tops together. Use masking tape to secure them as they dry. Join the top to the base in the same way.

STONE BRIDGE

Walla Brook bridge on Dartmoor is one of the oldest stone bridges in Britain. Bridges make travelling easier, safer and more direct. The first bridges were made by placing tree trunks across rivers, or by laying flat stones in shallow streams.

SAILING BOATS

Skin-covered boats called *umiak* were used by the Inuit of North America. The figure at the back is the helmsman, whose job is to steer the boat. The other figures are rowing the oars. The ancient Egyptians were among the first people to have sailing boats – for moving around on the River Nile.

KAYAK FRAME

This wooden frame for a kayak was made by an Inuit fisherman. It has been built without any nails. The joints were lashed together with strips of leather. Canoes like this have been in use for thousands of years.

Inuit kayaks give clues about how Stone Age boats may have looked. The outsides were covered with skin.

3 Draw three circles the size of the holes in the top, with smaller circles inside. Cut them out. Make clay rings the same size.

4 Cover the clay and the card rings with double-sided tape. These rings form the seats where the paddlers will sit.

5 Cover your canoe with chamois leather, leaving holes for seats. Glue it tightly in place so that all the cardboard is covered.

6 Use a needle and thread to sew up the edges of the leather on the top of the canoe. Position and fix the seats and oars.

Egyptian Sailpower

THE ANCIENT EGYPTIANS were not great seafarers, although their ships did sail through the Mediterranean and the Red Sea, and may even have reached India. Generally, though, they mostly kept to coastal waters and became experts at river travel. The River Nile was Egypt's main road, and all kinds of boats travelled up and down. Simple boats made from papyrus reed were used for fishing and hunting. Barges transported stones to temple building sites, ferries carried people and animals across the river. There were trading vessels and royal pleasure

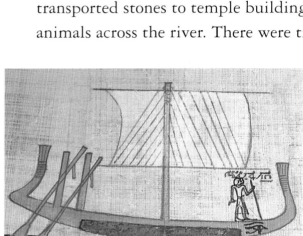

boats. Egypt had little timber, so wooden ships had to be built from cedar imported from Lebanon in the eastern Mediterranean.

THE FINAL VOYAGE

Archaeologists have found many well-preserved pictures and models of boats in tombs. People believed that the boats carried the mummified body of a pharaoh to its final resting place on the west bank of the Nile, and carried the dead person's spirit into the Underworld.

ALL ALONG THE NILE

Wooden sailing boats with graceful, triangular sails can still be seen on the River Nile today. They carry goods and people up and down the river. The design of the *felucca* has changed since the time of the ancient Egyptians. The sails on early boats were tall, upright and narrow. Later designs were broader, like the ones shown above. In Egypt, most people lived in the fertile valley of the River Nile. The river has always been the main route of communication and transport.

MAKE A BOAT

You will need: a large bundle of straw 30cm long, scissors, string, balsa wood, red and yellow card, pva glue and brush.

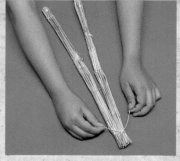

1 Divide the straw into five equal bundles and then cut three of them down to 15cm in length. Tie all five bundles securely at both ends and in the middle, as shown.

2 Take the two long bundles and tie them together at one end as shown. These bundles will form the outer frame of the boat. Put them to one side.

3 Next take the three short bundles of straw and bind them together at both ends. These will form the inner surface of the straw boat.

STEERING ROUND SAND BANKS

A wooden tomb model shows a boat from 1800BC with high, curved ends. Long steering oars kept the boat on course through the powerful currents of the flooding river. Timber was the main material for building large boats, but designs were similar to those of the simple reed vessels used for fishing.

FINAL VOYAGE

These boats are making a pilgrimage to Abydos. This was the city of Osiris, the god of death and rebirth. Mummies were taken here by boat. Ships and boats played a major part in the religious beliefs of the Egyptians. Ra the Sun god travelled on a boat across the sky to bring in each new day. In October 1991, a fleet of 12 boats dating from about 3000BC was found at Abydos near Memphis. The boats were up to 30m long and had been buried beneath the desert sands. They are the oldest surviving large ships in the world.

SIGN OF THE NORTH

The hieroglyph below means boat. It looks a bit like the papyrus reed vessels. This sign later came to mean north. Boats floated downstream with the current from south to north, and used sail power to travel the other way.

Early boats were made from papyrus reeds. These were bound with string made from reed fibres.

4 Next push the short bundles into the centre of the long pair firmly. Tie the bundles together with string at one end, as shown.

5 Bring the rear of the long pair of bundles together and tie them securely, as shown. Bind the whole boat together with string.

6 Thread a string lengthwise from one end to the other. The tension on this string should give the high curved prow and stern of your boat.

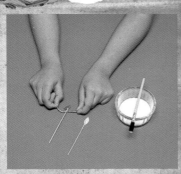

7 Finally, cut the card and glue it to the balsa sticks to make the boat's paddle and harpoon. Boats like these were used for fishing and hunting hippos.

Sailing in the Mediterranean

Galleys were sailed and rowed in Mediterranean waters for hundreds of years, from the heyday of Phoenician traders around 1000–572bc to the merchant galleys of Venice in the 1400s. Roman galleys were very similar to the earlier Greek vessels. When the wind was favourable, a big, square sail could be set for extra speed. Continuous power, though – whatever the weather – and manoeuvrability in battle – came from one or more rows of oars. A standard Roman war galley had 270 oarsmen below deck.

Most goods, especially heavy cargoes of food or building materials, were moved around the Roman Empire by water. Barges were used on rivers.

CONTAINERS
A large pottery jar called an amphora is being taken from one ship to another. Merchant ships were deeper, heavier and slower than galleys. They had bigger sails and longer oars. They were usually sailed, as they were too heavy to be rowed.

AT THE DOCKS
This wall painting from the port of Ostia shows a Roman merchant ship being loaded. Heavy sacks of grain are being carried on board. You can see the two large steering oars at the stern (rear) of the ship.

Seafaring in the Mediterranean was dangerous, mainly because of storms and piracy. The Greeks built the first lighthouse at Alexandria around 300bc, and the Romans built many around their empire.

ROLLING ON THE RIVER
Wine and other liquids were sometimes stored in barrels. These were transported by river barges, like the one in this carving. Barrels of wine would be hauled from the vineyards of Germany or southern France to the nearest seaport.

MAKE AN AMPHORA
You will need: large sheet of thin card, ruler, two pencils, scissors, corrugated cardboard – two circles of 10cm and 20cm in diameter, two strips of 40cm x 30cm and another large piece, masking tape, pva glue, old newspaper, paintbrush, reddish-brown acrylic paint, water pot.

1 Cut two pieces of card – 5cm and 38cm in depth. Tape the short piece to the small circle. Curl the long piece to make the neck. Make two holes in the side and tape it to the large circle.

2 Roll up the strips of corrugated cardboard. Bend them, as shown, fitting one end to the hole in the neck and the other to the cardboard. Fix in place with glue and tape.

3 Cut a piece of card, 40cm square. Roll it into a cylinder shape. Cut four lines, 10cm long, at one end, so it can be tapered into a point, as shown. Bind with tape.

SAILING OFF TO BATTLE

A Roman war galley leaves harbour on its way to battle. A helmsman controlled a war galley's steering and shouted orders down to the oarsmen below deck. Slaves manned the oars, and there was a separate fighting force on board. This galley has three banks (layers) of oars and is called a trireme (meaning three oars). An underwater battering ram stuck out from the bow (front) of Greek and Roman war galleys. During battle, the mast was lowered, as the ship was easier to manoeuvre under oarpower. The galley rammed the enemy ship to disable it. Then the soldiers boarded to fight man to man.

In the ancient world, amphorae were used to transport wine and oil and fish sauce. Amphorae could be easily stacked in the ship's hold. Layers of brushwood provided padding.

4 To give the amphora a more solid base, roll up a cone of corrugated cardboard and stick it around the tapered end. Push a pencil into the end, as shown. Tape in position.

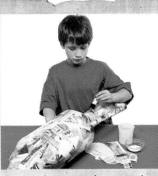

5 Stick the neck on to the main body. Cover the whole piece with strips of newspaper brushed on with glue. Leave to dry. Repeat until you have built up a thick layer.

6 When the paper is dry, paint the amphora. Roman amphorae were made of clay, so use a reddish-brown paint to make yours look like it is clay. Leave to dry.

Overland in China

HEADING OUT WEST
Chinese horsemen escort the camels of a caravan (trading expedition). The traders are about to set out along the Silk Road. This trading route ran all the way from Chang'an (Xian) in China to Europe and the lands of the Mediterranean.

THE ANCIENT CHINESE EMPIRE was linked by a network of roads used only by the army, officials and royal messengers. A special carriageway was reserved for the emperor. Ordinary people travelled along dusty or muddy routes and tracks.

China's mountainous landscape and large number of rivers meant that engineers became expert at bridge-building. Suspension bridges of rope and bamboo were built from about AD1 onwards. A bridge suspended from iron chains crossed the Chang Jiang (Yangzi River) as early as AD580. A stone arch bridge of AD615 still stands today at Zhouxian in Hebei province.

Most people travelled by foot, and porters carried great loads on their backs or balanced on shoulder poles. Single-wheeled barrows were useful too, 1,000 years before they were invented in the West. China's small native ponies were interbred with larger, stronger horses from central Asia sometime after 100BC. This provided fast, powerful mounts that were suitable for messengers and officials, and could also pull chariots and carriages. Mules and camels were the animals used on the trade routes of the north, while shaggy yaks carried loads in the high mountains. Carts were usually hauled by oxen.

RIDING ON HORSEBACK
A Chinese nobleman from about 2,000 years ago reins in his elegant horse. Breaking in the horse would have been difficult, as the rider has no stirrups and could easily be unseated. Metal stirrups were in general use in China by AD302. They provided more stability and helped the rider control his horse.

CARRIED BY HAND
A lazy landowner of the Qing dynasty travels around his estates. Wealthy people were often carried in a litter (a portable chair). An umbrella shades the landowner from the heat of the summer sun.

CAMEL POWER
Bactrian (two-humped) camels were originally bred in central Asia. They could endure extremes of heat and cold and travel for long distances without water. This toughness made them ideal for transporting goods through the mountains and deserts of the Silk Road.

HAN CARRIAGE
During the Han dynasty (202BC–AD 220), three-horse carriages were used by the imperial family only. This carving from a tomb brick probably shows a messenger carrying an important order from the emperor.

TRAVELLING IN STYLE
Han dynasty government officials travelled in stylish horse-drawn carriages. New breeds of large strong horses became a status symbol for the rich and powerful. The animals were considered celestial (heavenly). The Han civilization developed around the Huang He (Yellow River). Han people invented the chariot by 1500BC, around 500 years later than in Mesopotamia.

The Chinese Afloat

IN FULL SAIL
Junks were a type of sailing vessel used by merchants in the East and South China seas. They were also used by pirates. The China seas could be blue and peaceful, but they were often whipped into a fury by typhoons (tropical storms).

ROM EARLY IN CHINA'S history, the country's rivers, lakes and man-made canals were its main highways. Fishermen propelled small wooden boats with a single oar or pole at the stern. These small boats were often roofed with mats, like the sampans (meaning 'three planks') still seen today. Large, wooden, ocean-sailing ships called junks were either keeled or flat-bottomed, with a high stern and square bows. Matting sails were stiffened with strips of bamboo.

By the 1st century AD, the Chinese had built the first ships with rudders instead of steering oars, and soon went on to make ships with several masts. In the 1400s, admirals Zheng He and Wang Jinghong led expeditions to South-east Asia, India, Arabia and East Africa. The flagship of their 300-strong naval fleet was over five times the size of the largest European ships of the time.

RIVER TRAFFIC
All sorts of small trading boats were sailed or rowed along China's rivers in the 1850s. River travel had always been difficult and could be dangerous. The Huang He (Yellow River) often flooded and changed course. The upper parts of China's longest river, the Chang Jiang (Yangzi River), were rocky and had powerful currents.

MAKE A SAMPAN

You will need: ruler, pencil, thick and thin card, scissors, glue and brush, masking tape, 6 wooden barbecue sticks, string, thin yellow paper, paint (black, dark brown), paintbrush, water pot.

39cm
1cm — Runner A (x2)

33.5cm
Side B (x2) — 5cm
15cm

Base C (x2) — 7cm — Base D
15cm — 18cm
7cm — Floor E — 4cm — Floor F (x2)
10cm — 7cm — Edge G (x2) — 1cm
6.5cm

Cut pieces B, C, D and G from thick card. Cut pieces A, E, and F from thin card.

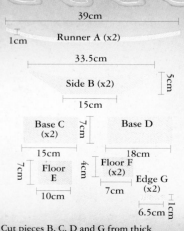

1 Glue base pieces C and D to side B, as shown. Hold the pieces with masking tape while the glue dries. When dry, remove the masking tape.

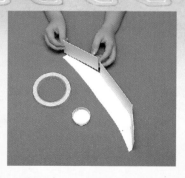

2 Glue remaining side B to the boat. Stick runner A pieces to top of the sides. Make sure the ends jut out 2.5cm at the front and back of the boat.

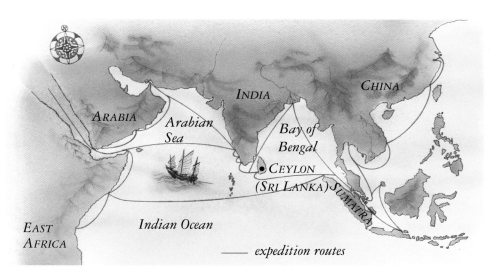

FISHERMEN'S FEASTS

Seas, lakes and rivers were an important food source in imperial China. Drying fish was often the only way to preserve it in the days before refrigeration. Dried fish made strong-tasting sauces and soups. Popular seafoods included crabs, prawns and squid.

dried fish

dried squid

THE VOYAGES OF ZHENG HE

Chinese admirals Zheng He and Wang Jinghong carried out seven fantastic voyages of exploration between 1405 and 1433. This map shows how far and wide they travelled on these expeditions. Their impressive fleets included over 60 ships crewed by about 27,000 seamen, officers and interpreters. The biggest of their vessels was 147m long and 60m wide.

THE FISHING TRIP

A fisherman poles his boat across the river in the 1500s. The bird shown in the picture is a tamed cormorant, used for catching the fish. The cormorant was normally attached to a line, with a ring around its neck to prevent it from swallowing the fish.

To add the finishing touch to your sampan, make a boatman and oar to propel the vessel through the waterways.

3 Glue floor E to centre of base. Add floor F pieces to the ends of the base, as shown. Stick edge G pieces in between the ends of the runners.

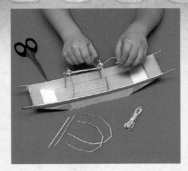

4 Bend 2 barbecue sticks into 10cm high arches. Cut 2 more sticks into five 10cm struts. Glue and tie 2 struts to sides of arches and 1 to the top.

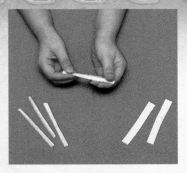

5 Repeat step 4 to make a second roof. To make roof matting, cut thin yellow paper into 1cm x 10cm strips. Fold strips in half and stick to roofs.

6 Paint boat and roofs. Allow to dry. Glue the matting strips to the roofs, as shown. When the glue is dry, place roofs inside the boat.

Over the Mountains of Japan

J APAN IS A RUGGED and mountainous country. Until the 1900s, the only routes through the countryside were narrow, winding tracks. Paths and fragile wooden bridges across deep gullies and streams were often swept away by landslides or floods.

During the Heian period (from around AD794), wealthy warriors rode fine horses, while important officials, wealthy women, children and priests travelled in lightweight wood and bamboo carts. The carts were pulled by oxen and fitted with screens and curtains for privacy. If the route was impassable for ox-carts, wealthy people were carried on palanquins (lightweight portable boxes or litters). Ordinary people usually travelled on foot.

During the Tokugawa period (1600–1868) the shoguns (military rulers) encouraged new road building as a way of increasing trade and keeping control of their lands. The Eastern Sea Road ran for 480km between Kyoto and the shogun's capital, Edo, and took 20-30 days to travel on foot. Some people said it was the busiest road in the world.

BEASTS OF BURDEN
A weary mother rests with her child and ox during their journey. You can see that the ox is loaded up with heavy bundles. Ordinary people could not afford horses, so oxen were used to carry heavy loads or to pull carts.

SHOULDER HIGH
Noblewomen on palanquins (litters) are being taken by porters across a deep river. Some women have decided to disembark so that they can be carried across the river. Palanquins were used in Japan right up to the Tokugawa period (1600–1868). Daimyos (warlords) and their wives might be carried the whole journey to or from the capital city of Edo in a palanquin.

HUGGING THE COASTLINE

Ships sail into harbour at Tempozan, Osaka. The marks on the sails show the company that owned them. Cargo between the shogun's city of Edo and Osaka was mostly carried by ships that hugged the coastline.

CARRYING CARGO

Little cargo-boats, such as these at Edobashi in Edo, carried goods along rivers or around the coast. They were driven through the water by men rowing with oars or pushing against the river bed with a long pole.

STEEP MOUNTAIN PATHS

Travellers on mountain paths hoped to find shelter for the night in villages, temples or monasteries. It could take all day to walk 16km along rough mountain tracks.

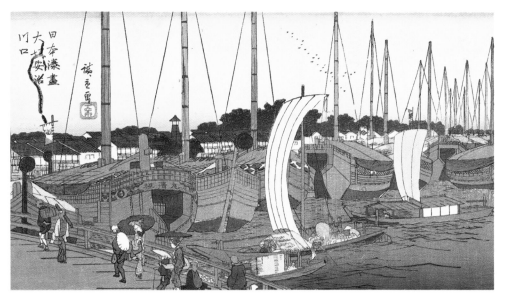

IN THE HARBOUR

Sea-going sailing ships, laden with cargo, are shown here at anchor in the harbour of Osaka, an important port in south-central Japan. In front of them you can see smaller river-boats with tall sails. Some families both lived and worked on river-boats.

Viking Specialities

IT WAS OFTEN QUICKER for the Vikings to travel around the coast than over the icy mountains. However, they used horses for carrying baggage and pulling wheeled carts and wagons over their wooden causeways. Sledges hauled goods over grass as well as ice and snow. The Vikings became best known, however, for their shipbuilding skills. Longships were designed for ocean voyages and warfare. They were up to 23m long but were shallow enough to row on rivers. A single oak beam was used for the keel – the backbone of the ship. Planks were caulked (made watertight) with wool or animal hair and coated with a tar made of pine resin. Oar holes ran the length of the ship, and there was a broad steering oar at the stern (back). The large square or rectangular sail was made of heavy woollen or linen cloth.

The Vikings also made broad-beamed cargo and trading vessels and small rowing and sailing boats.

DRAGON SHIPS
The hulls were clinker-built. This means that long, wedge shaped strakes (planks) were nailed to the frame so that they overlapped.

MAKE A SLEDGE

You will need: cardboard, balsa wood, ruler, pencil, craft knife, red acrylic paint, paint brush, brown construction paper, pva glue, glue brush, paper fasteners, masking tape, red string, fur fabric.

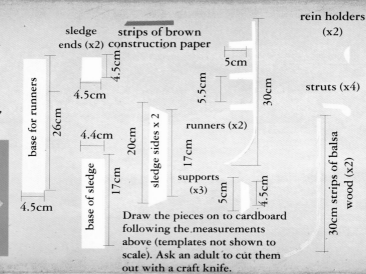

sledge ends (x2) strips of brown construction paper

rein holders (x2)

base for runners — 26cm

4.5cm

4.5cm

4.5cm

sledge sides x 2 — 20cm

base of sledge — 17cm

4.4cm

17cm

5.5cm

5cm

30cm

struts (x4)

runners (x2) — 17cm

supports (x3) — 5cm

4.5cm

30cm strips of balsa wood (x2)

Draw the pieces on to cardboard following the measurements above (templates not shown to scale). Ask an adult to cut them out with a craft knife.

1 Paint one side of each of the 9 pieces that will form the top of the sledge, as shown. When they have dried, turn them over and paint the other side.

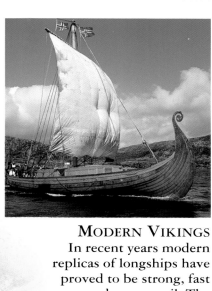

MODERN VIKINGS

In recent years modern replicas of longships have proved to be strong, fast and easy to sail. The planking bends well to the waves and the ships are light enough to be hauled overland.

PUTTING TO SEA

A longship put to sea with a crew of 30 or more fighting men. In Greek and Roman galleys, there was a separate fighting force. The Vikings, though, were both warriors and sailors. They sometimes slung their round shields along the side of the ship.

SHIPS' TIMBERS

In the Viking Age, much of northern Europe was still densely forested. In most places there was no shortage of timber for building or repairing longships. Oak was always the shipbuilders' first choice of wood, followed by pine, beech and ash.

beech

oak

Many Viking sledges were designed to be pulled by horses and were often finely carved.

2 Cut several strips of brown construction paper. Arrange them to form diamond patterns along the sides of the sledge. Trim and glue in place.

3 Ask an adult to make cuts with a craft knife. Push paper fasteners through to form patterns. Glue the top of the sledge. Hold it together with masking tape.

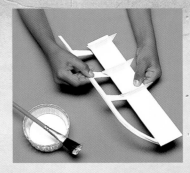

4 While you wait for the top to dry, glue the 8 pieces that form the base of the sledge together. Glue the 2 rein holders on the top of the base.

5 Paint the base red. When it is dry, brush plenty of glue on to it and carefully stick on the top. Leave it to dry. Attach the rein and trim with fur fabric.

Wheel-less in Mesoamerica

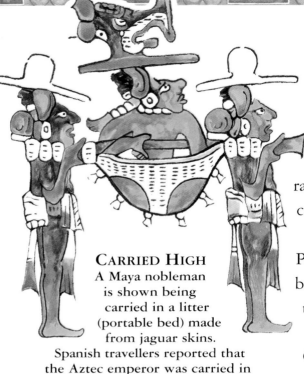

THE AZTEC AND MAYA PEOPLE of Central America knew about wheels and built an intricate system of roads – but they did not make wheeled transport of any kind. Carriages and carts would not have been able to travel through dense rainforests, along steep, narrow mountain tracks or the raised causeways that linked many cities.

Most people travelled on foot, carrying goods on their backs. Porters carried heavy loads with the help of a *tumpline*. This was a broad band of cloth that went across their foreheads and under the bundles on their backs, leaving their arms free. Rulers and nobles were carried in portable beds, called litters.

On rivers and lakes, Mesoamericans used simple dug-out boats. Maya sailors travelled in huge wooden canoes that were able to make long voyages, even in the rough, open sea.

CARRIED HIGH

A Maya nobleman is shown being carried in a litter (portable bed) made from jaguar skins. Spanish travellers reported that the Aztec emperor was carried in the same way. When the emperor walked, blankets were spread in front of him so that his feet did not touch the ground.

MEN OR MONSTERS?

Until the Spaniards arrived with horses in 1519, there were no animals big and strong enough to ride in the Mesoamerican lands. There were horses in America in prehistoric times, but they died out around 10,000BC. When the Aztecs saw the Spanish riding, they thought the animals were monsters – half man, half beast.

MAKE A WHEELED DOG

You will need: board, self-drying clay, 4 lengths of thin dowel about 5cm long and 2 lengths about 7cm long, water bowl, thick card, scissors, pva glue, glue brush, paintbrush, paint, masking tape.

1 Roll a large piece of clay into a fat sausage to form the dog's body. Push the 5cm pieces of dowel into the body to make the legs. Leave to dry.

2 Cover the dowel legs with clay, extending the clay 2cm beyond the end of the dowel. Make a hole at the end of each leg with a piece of dowel. Leave to dry.

3 Push the dowel through the holes in the legs to join them horizontally. Make the dog's head and ears from clay. Join them to the body using water.

HARDWORKING PORTERS

This engraving from the 1900s shows Aztec slaves and commoners carrying loads for Spanish conquerors. Being a porter was very hard work. They were expected to cover up to 100km per day, carrying about 25–30kg on their backs. Like most Mesoamerican people, they travelled these long distances barefoot.

BY BOAT

The city of Tenochtitlan was built on artificial islands on a lake. Transport around the city was by flat-bottomed boat. The boats ferried people and transported fruits and vegetables to market. Dug-out canoes made from hollowed-out tree trunks were popular too.

AZTEC WATERWAYS

The Aztecs paddled their canoes and flat-bottomed boats on Lake Texcoco. Today most of this lake has dried up. The lakeside *chinampas*, where they grew food and flowers, have almost disappeared. This photograph shows modern punts sailing along one of the last remaining Aztec waterways between the few *chinampas* that survive.

Toys such as this dog are proof that the wheel was known in Mesoamerica. Wheeled vehicles were not suitable for rugged Mesoamerican land.

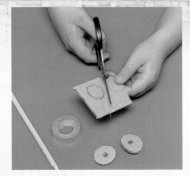

4 Cut four circles 3.5cm in diameter from card to make wheels. Pierce a hole in the centre of each. Make the holes big enough for the dowel to fit through

5 Make four wheels from clay, the same size as the card wheels. Glue the clay and card wheels together. Make holes through the clay wheels and leave to dry.

6 Paint the dog's head, body, legs and wheels with Aztec patterns. When the paint is dry, give the dog a thin coat of pva glue to act as a varnish.

7 Fit the wheels on to the ends of the dowels that pass through the dog's legs. Wrap strips of masking tape around the ends to stop the wheels falling off.

WHEEL-LESS IN MESOAMERICA 23

Arctic Travel

DURING THE WINTER, the surface of the Arctic Ocean freezes and snow covers the land. In the past, sledges were the most common way of travelling over the ice and snow. They were made from bone or timber lashed together with strips of hide or whale sinew. They glided over the snow on runners made from walrus tusks or wood. Arctic sledges had to be light enough to be pulled by animals, yet strong enough to carry an entire family and its belongings. In North America, huskies pulled the sledges. In Siberia and Scandinavia, however, reindeer were used.

From ancient times, Arctic peoples have needed skis and snowshoes to travel over snow. Skis are thought to have been invented by the Saami people of Lapland more than 3,500 years ago. Snowshoes enabled Arctic hunters to stalk prey without sinking into deep snowdrifts.

REINDEER SLEDGES
Three reindeer stand by a family and their sledge in Siberia. In Arctic Russia and Scandinavia, reindeer were commonly used to pull sledges. Small, narrow sledges carried just one person. Larger, wider models could take much heavier loads.

HITCHING A DOG TEAM
A husky team struggles up a hill in eastern Greenland. Traditionally, the traces (reins) that connected the dogs to the sledge were made of walrus hide. Different Arctic cultures used one of two arrangements to hitch the dogs together. Some people hitched them in the shape of a fan. Others hitched the dogs in pairs in a long line.

MAKE A MODEL SLEDGE

You will need: thick card, balsa wood, ruler, pencil, scissors, pva glue, glue brush, masking tape, compass, barbecue stick, string, shammy leather, brown paint, paint brush, water pot.

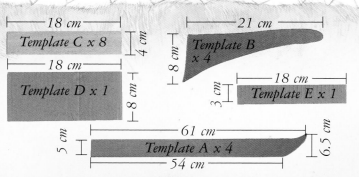

← 18 cm →	← 21 cm →
Template C x 8 (4 cm)	Template B x 4 (8 cm)
← 18 cm →	← 18 cm →
Template D x 1 (8 cm)	Template E x 1 (3 cm)
← 61 cm → (5 cm)	
Template A x 4	(6.5 cm)
← 54 cm →	

Using the shapes above for reference, measure out the shapes on the card (use balsa wood for template C). Cut the shapes out using your scissors. You will need to make 4 A templates, 4 B templates, 8 C templates (balsa wood), 1 D template and 1 E template. Always remember to cut away from your body when using scissors.

1 Glue 2 A templates together. Repeat this for the other 2 A templates. Repeat this with the 4 B templates. Cover all the edges with masking tape.

SNOWSHOES

Snowshoes are used to walk across deep snowdrifts without sinking into the snow. They spread the person's weight across a large area. To make the snowshoe, thin, flexible birch saplings were steamed to make them supple. The saplings were then bent into the shape of the snowshoe frame. Some shoes were rounded but others were long and narrow. The netting was woven from long strips of animal hide.

birch sapling

rawhide thongs

snowshoes

MAN'S BEST FRIEND

This picture, painted around 1890, shows an Inuit hunter harnessing one of his huskies. Huskies were vital to Inuit society. On the hunt, the dogs helped to nose out seals hiding in their dens. They hauled heavy loads of meat back to camp.

SAAMI SKIS

The Saami have used skis for thousands of years. Early skis were made of wood and the undersides were covered with strips of reindeer skin. The hairs on the skin pointed backwards, giving the skier grip when walking uphill.

LET SLEEPING DOGS LIE

A husky's thick coat keeps it warm in temperatures as low as −50°C. These hardy animals can sleep peacefully in the fiercest of blizzards. The snow builds up against their fur and insulates them.

Inuit hunters used wooden sledges pulled by huskies to hunt for food over a large area. The wood was lashed together with animal hide or sinew.

2 Using a compass, make small holes along the top edge of the glued A templates. Use the end of a barbecue stick to make the holes a little larger.

3 Glue the balsa wood slats C in position over the holes along the A templates as shown above. You will need to use all 8 balsa wood slats.

4 Carefully glue the B templates and the E and D templates to the end of the sledge, as shown above. Allow to dry, then paint the model.

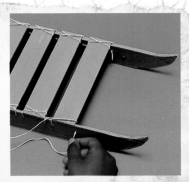

5 Thread string through the holes to secure the slats on each side. Decorate the sledge with a shammy-covered card box and secure it to the sledge.

Early Conflicts in Mesopotamia

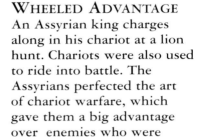

THE CITY-STATES of Mesopotamia were frequently at war with one another. Usually, the disputes were local affairs over pieces of land or the ownership of canals. Later, powerful kings created empires and warred with foreign countries. King Sargon of Agade, for example, subdued all the cities of Sumer and then conquered great cities in northern Syria. Assyria and Babylonia were often at war in the first millennium BC. The walls of Assyrian palaces were decorated with reliefs (painted carvings) that celebrate battle scenes.

The Mesopotamians were among the first people to invent the wheel. They put this to good use in chariot warfare and wheeled siege machines.

WHEELED ADVANTAGE
An Assyrian king charges along in his chariot at a lion hunt. Chariots were also used to ride into battle. The Assyrians perfected the art of chariot warfare, which gave them a big advantage over enemies who were fighting on foot.

IN THE BEGINNING
A model of a very early chariot, about 4,000 years old, shows the first wheel designs of solid wood. By the time of the Assyrian Empire, about 900-600 BC, war chariots had spoked wooden wheels with metal rims.

THE KING'S GUARDS
A panel from the palace of the Persian kings at Susa shows a long procession of king's guards. The guards are armed with spears, and carry quivers full of arrows. King Cyrus of Persia conquered Babylon in 539BC.

MAKE A CHARIOT
You will need: pen, cardboard, scissors, paints and paintbrushes, flour, water and newspaper to make papier mâché, glue, masking tape, 2 x dowel 16cm long, card tubes, needle, 4 cocktail sticks.

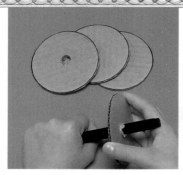

1 Cut four circles about 7cm in width out of the card. Use the scissors to make a hole in the centre of each circle. Enlarge the holes with a pen.

2 Cut out two sides for the chariot 12cm long x 8cm high as shown, one back 9 x 8cm, one front 9 x 15cm, one top 9 x 7cm and one base 12 x 9cm.

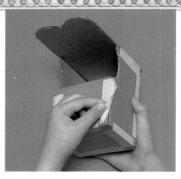

3 Trim the top of the front to two curves as shown. Stick the side pieces to the front and back using masking tape. Stick on the base and top.

SLINGS AND ARROWS

Assyrian foot-soldiers used rope slings and stone balls the size of modern tennis balls. Others fired arrows while sheltering behind tall wicker shields. They wore helmets of bronze or iron and were protected by metal scale armour and leather boots.

GOING INTO BATTLE

Sumerian chariot drivers charge into battle. A soldier armed with spears stands on the footplate of each chariot ready to jump off and fight. They are all protected by thick leather cloaks and helmets. The chariots were drawn by onegars (wild asses).

STORMING A CITY

Many Assyrian fighting methods can be seen in the palace reliefs at the city of Nimrud. In this scene, the Assyrians storm an enemy city which stands on a hill. A siege engine with spears projecting from the front breaks down the walls. Attacking soldiers climbed the walls with the help of siege ladders, and they were protected by archers.

Your chariot copies a clay model made in northern Mesopotamia over 4,000 years ago.

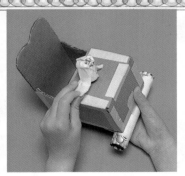

4 Roll up a piece of newspaper to make a cylinder shape 3cm long, and attach it to the chariot. Attach the cardboard tubes to the bottom of the chariot.

5 Mix a paste of flour and water. Dip newspaper strips into the paste to make papier mâché. Cover the chariot with layers of papier mâché. Leave to dry.

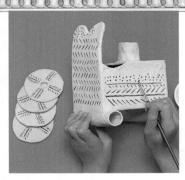

6 Paint the whole chariot cream. Add detail using brown paint. Paint the wheels, too. Make a hole with the needle in each end of the dowels.

7 Insert a cocktail stick in the dowel, add a wheel and insert into the tube. Fix another wheel and stick to the other end. Repeat with the other wheels.

Indian Armies

ONFLICT WAS A FACT OF LIFE in India from the time when people invaded from central Asia around 1750BC. At first, tribes fought and stole each others' cattle. Gradually, empires grew and warfare became more elaborate. By the time of the emperor Ashoka in 250BC, armies were divided into four parts – infantry (footsoldiers), cavalry (horses), chariots and elephants. The infantry was the core of all Indian armies, but was often made up of poorly trained peasants. Elephants were symbols of royalty, majesty and prestige.

In the first millennium AD, when the Turks invaded, chariots became less important. This was because the Turks had excellent horses and could use bows on horseback. Soon, all Indian armies copied them and developed a top-grade cavalry. The first recorded use of gunpowder in Indian warfare was in the 1400s. Later, the Mughals combined field artillery (guns) with cavalry and elephants.

UNEQUAL CONTEST
A mounted warrior and a footsoldier attack each other. From the 1200s, nobles preferred to fight on horseback. Footsoldiers faced a height disadvantage when fighting mounted soldiers. The horsemen could also use swords as well as bows.

SUPERIOR WARRIOR
A Mongol warrior draws his bow and aims behind him as he rides. The Mongols were great fighters, especially on horseback. In 1398, they devastated Delhi and took many of its citizens as slaves.

MUGHAL HELMET
You will need: strips of newspaper, flour and water or wallpaper paste, bowl, inflated balloon, scissors, fine sandpaper, thin card, sticky tape or pva glue, gold and black paint, paintbrushes, 20 x 10 cm piece of black card, ruler.

1 Soak the newspaper in the paste or flour and water. Cover half the balloon with three layers of newspaper. Leave to dry between layers.

2 When dry, burst the balloon and remove it. Smooth edges of helmet with sandpaper. Wrap a strip of card around the base. Fix with tape or glue.

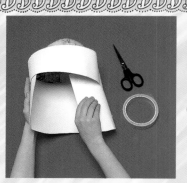

3 Place a longer piece of card inside the helmet. It should be long enough to cover your ears and neck. Glue or tape it into position and trim to fit.

FORTIFIED CHAIR

A king at war travels in a fortified howdah (chair) on an elephant's back. The combination of howdah and elephant was like the armoured tank of modern warfare. The best elephants for army use came mainly from eastern and southern India, and Sri Lanka.

LIGHT PROTECTION

A Hindu warrior on horseback prepares to hurl his spear. Warriors had little armour besides shields. They often wore ornaments and lucky charms.

BEST WEAPON

The Hindu footsoldier's favoured weapons were the bow and arrow, and the sword. However, they also fought with maces, lances, spears and daggers.

FINE WEAPONRY

This Mughal dagger handle is inlaid with gold and jewels. Weapons were often crafted from the finest materials.

A Mughal warrior wore a plumed helmet to protect his head in battle.

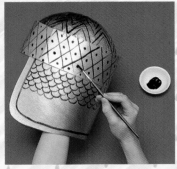

4 Paint the entire helmet with two coats of gold paint, using a medium-sized paintbrush. Allow the paint to dry completely between coats.

5 Add detail with black paint and a fine paintbrush. You could use a Mughal pattern like the one shown here, or design your own.

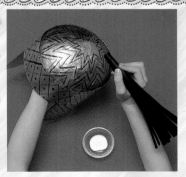

6 Cut narrow slits 5 mm apart in the black card. Leave 5 cm uncut at the bottom of the card. Cover this patch with glue and roll the card up tightly.

7 When the glue is dry, fix the plume to the top of your helmet with glue, or you can cut a small hole in the helmet and push the plume through.

Shoguns and Samurai

BETWEEN 1185 AND 1600 there were a great many wars throughout Japan. Rival warlords fought to become shogun – the title held by the military ruler. Some former emperors also tried, unsuccessfully, to restore imperial rule. During this troubled time in Japanese history, emperors, shoguns and daimyo all relied on armies of well-trained samurai to fight their battles. The samurai were highly trained warriors from noble families. Members of each samurai army were bound by a solemn oath, sworn to their lord. They stayed loyal from a sense of honour – and because their lord gave them rich rewards. The civil wars ended around 1600, when the Tokugawa dynasty of shoguns came to power. From this time onwards, samurai spent less time fighting, and served instead as officials and business managers.

RIDING OFF TO WAR
Painted in 1772, this samurai general is in full armour. A samurai's horse had to be fast, agile and strong enough to carry the full weight of the samurai, his armour and his weapons.

TACHI
Swords were a favourite weapon of the samurai. This long sword is called a *tachi*. It was made in the 1500s for ceremonial use by a samurai.

METAL HELMET
Samurai helmets like this were made from curved metal panels, carefully fitted together, and decorated with elaborate patterns. The jutting peak protected the wearer's face and the nape-guard covered the back of the neck. This helmet dates from around 1380.

SAMURAI HELMET
You will need: *thick card, pin, string, felt-tip pen, ruler, scissors, tape measure, newspaper, bowl, water, pva glue, balloon, petroleum jelly, pencil, modelling clay, bradawl, paper, gold card, paints, brush, water pot, glue brush, masking tape, paper fasteners, 2 x 20cm lengths of cord.*

1 Draw a circle 18cm in diameter on card using the pin, string and felt-tip pen. Using the same method, draw two larger circles 20cm and 50cm.

2 Draw a line across the centre of the three circles using the ruler and felt-tip pen. Draw tabs in the middle semi-circle. Add two flaps as shown.

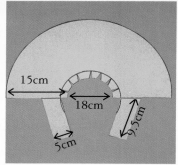

3 Now cut out the neck protector piece completely, as shown above. Make sure that you cut around the tabs and flaps exactly.

15cm
18cm
2.5cm
5cm

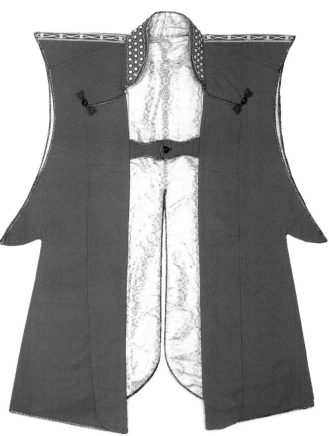

SURCOAT FINERY

For festivals, ceremonies and parades samurai wore surcoats (long, loose tunics) over their armour. Surcoats were made from fine, glossy silks, dyed in rich colours. This example was made during the Tokugawa period (1600–1868). Surcoats were often decorated with family crests. These were originally used to identify soldiers in battle, but later became badges of high rank.

PROTECTIVE CLOTHING

This fine suit of samurai armour dates from the Tokugawa period (1600–1868). Armour gave the samurai life-saving protection in battle. High-ranking warriors wore suits of plate armour, made of iron panels, laced or riveted together and combined with panels of chain mail or rawhide. Lower-ranking soldiers called *ashigaru* wore thinner, lightweight armour, made of small metal plates. A full suit of samurai armour could weigh anything up to 18kg.

MAKING BOWS

Japanese craftworkers are busy at work making bows, around 1600. The bow was the Japanese warrior's most ancient weapon. Bows were made of wood and bamboo and fired many different kinds of arrow.

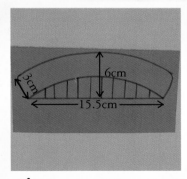

4 Draw the peak template piece on another piece of card. Follow the measurements shown in the picture. Cut out the peak template.

5 To make papier-mâché, tear the newspaper into small strips. Fill the bowl with 1 part PVA glue to 3 parts water. Add the newspaper strips.

6 Blow up the balloon to the size of your head. Cover with petroleum jelly. Build up three papier-mâché layers on the top and sides. Leave to dry between layers.

7 When dry, pop the balloon and trim. Ask a friend to make a mark on either side of your head.

Instructions for the helmet continue on the next page...

Honour Among Samurai

SAMURAI WERE HIGHLY TRAINED WARRIORS who dedicated their lives to fighting for their lords. However, being a samurai involved more than just fighting. The ideal samurai was supposed to follow a strict code of behaviour, governing all aspects of his life. This code was called *bushido* (the way of the warrior). *Bushido* called for skill, self-discipline, bravery, loyalty, honour, honesty, obedience and, at times, self-sacrifice. It taught that it was nobler to die fighting than to run away and survive.

Many samurai warriors followed the religious teachings of Zen, a branch of the Buddhist faith. Zen was introduced into Japan by two monks, Eisai and Dogen, who went to China to study in the 1100s and 1200s and brought Zen practices back with them. Teachers of Zen encouraged their followers to meditate (to free the mind of all thoughts) in order to achieve enlightenment.

THE TAKEDA FAMILY
The famous daimyo (warlord) Takeda Shingen (1521–1573), fires an arrow using his powerful bow. The influential Takeda family owned estates in Kai province near the city of Edo and kept a large private army of samurai warriors. Takeda Shingen fought a series of wars with his near neighbour, Uesugi Kenshin. However, in 1581, the Takeda were defeated by the army of General Nobunaga.

SWORDSMEN
It took young samurai many years to master the skill of swordsmanship. They were trained by master swordsmen. The best swords, made of strong, springy steel, were even given their own names.

8 Place clay under the pencil marks. Make two holes – one above and one below each pencil mark – with a bradawl. Repeat on the other side.

9 Fold a piece of A4 paper and draw a horn shape on to it following the design shown above. Cut out this shape so that you have an identical pair of horns.

10 Take a piece of A4 size gold card. Place your paper horns on to the gold card and draw around them. Carefully cut the horns out of the card.

11 Paint the papier-mâché helmet brown. Paint a weave design on the neck protector and a cream block on each flap. Leave to dry.

OFF TO WAR
A samurai warrior (on horseback) and foot-soldiers set off for war. Samurai had to command and inspire confidence in others, so it was especially important for them to behave in a brave and honourable way.

MARTIAL ARTS
Several sports that people enjoy playing today have developed from samurai fighting skills. In aikido, players try to throw their opponent off-balance and topple them to the ground. In kendo, players fight one another with long swords made of split bamboo. They score points by managing to touch their opponent's body, not by cutting or stabbing them!

kendo   *aikido*

SURVIVAL SKILLS
Samurai had to know how to survive in wild countryside. Each man carried emergency rations of dried rice. He also used his fighting skills to hunt wild animals for food.

ZEN
The Buddhist monk Rinzai is shown in this Japanese brush and ink scroll-painting. Rinzai was a famous teacher of Zen ideas. Many pupils, including samurai, travelled to his remote monastery in the mountains to study with him.

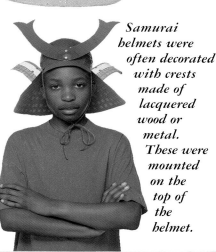

Samurai helmets were often decorated with crests made of lacquered wood or metal. These were mounted on the top of the helmet.

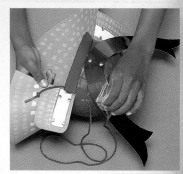

12 Bend back the tabs on the peak piece. Position it at the front of the helmet. Stick the tabs to the inside with glue. Hold in place with tape.

13 Now take the neck protector. Bend back the front flaps and the tabs. Glue the tabs to the helmet, as shown. Leave the helmet to dry.

14 Stick the horns to the front of the helmet. Use paper fasteners to secure, as shown. Decorate the ear flaps with paper fasteners.

15 Thread cord through one of the holes made in step 8. Tie a knot in the end. Thread the other end of the cord through the second hole. Repeat on the other side.

Greek Fighting Forces

ALL GREEK MEN were expected to fight in their city's army. In Sparta the army was on duty all year round. In other parts of Greece men gave up fighting in autumn so that they could bring in the harvest and make the wine. The only full-time soldiers were the personal bodyguards of a ruler and mercenaries who fought for anyone who paid them. Armies consisted mainly of hoplites (armoured infantry), cavalry (soldiers on horseback) and a group of foot soldiers armed with stones and bows and arrows. The hoplites engaged in hand-to-hand combt and were the most important fighting force. The cavalry was less effective because riders had no stirrups. This made charging with a lance impossible, as the rider would fall off on contact. Instead horsemen were used for scouting, harassing a beaten enemy and carrying messages.

HARD HELMET
This bronze helmet from the city of Corinth was fashioned to protect the face. It has guards for the cheeks and the bridge of the nose. Iron later replaced bronze as the main metal for weapons.

BOWMEN
The Greek army usually employed Scythian archers from north of the Black Sea to fight for them. Archers were useful for fighting in mountainous countryside if they were positioned above the enemy. Some Greek soldiers did fight with bows and arrows. They fought in small units known as *psiloi*. But most of the soldiers in these units could only afford simple missile weapons, such as a javelin or slings from which they shot stones.

WARRIOR GREAVES
You will need: clear film, bowl of water, plaster bandages, sheet of paper, kitchen paper, scissors, cord, gold paint, paintbrush.

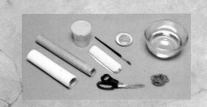

1 Ask a friend to help you with steps 1 to 3. Loosely cover both of your lower legs (from your ankle to the top of your knee) in clear film.

2 Soak each plaster bandage in water. Working from one side of your leg to the other, smooth the bandage over the front of each leg.

3 Carefully remove each greave. Set them on some paper. Dampen some kitchen paper and use it to smooth the greaves down. Leave them to dry.

A RARE SIGHT IN BATTLE

Chariots were not often used in Greek warfare. They could only be used on plains. There were usually two people in the chariot, one to drive it and the other to fight from the back.

FIGHTING FORCES

Tin and copper were used to make bronze, the main material for weapons and armour. Bronze is harder than pure copper and, unlike iron, does not rust. As there was no tin in Greece, it was imported from faraway lands.

copper   *tin*

MIDDLE CLASS FOOT SOLDIERS

The hoplite fighting force was made up of middle-class men who could afford to arm themselves. A hoplite's armoury consisted of a shield, helmet, spear, sword and greaves. Helmets were made of bronze and were usually crested with horsehair. The body was protected by a bronze cuirass – a one-piece breast- and back-plate. Underneath this, there was a leather cuirass. Shields were usually round and decorated with a symbol.

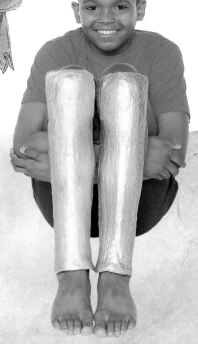

4 Trim the edges of the greaves, to make them look neat. Measure four lengths of cord to fit around your leg, below the knee and above the ankle.

5 Turn the greaves on to their front. Lay the cord in place at the point where you want to tie them to your leg. Fix them into place using wet bandages.

6 Leave the plaster bandages to dry, with the cord in place. Now paint each greave with gold paint. Once they are dry, tie them on.

Greaves were attached to the lower leg to protect it in battle. They were worn by hoplites.

Legions of Romans

THE ARMY OF THE EARLY ROMAN EMPIRE was divided into 28 groups called legions. Each of these numbered about 5,500 soldiers. The legion included mounted troops and foot-soldiers. They were organized into cohorts of about 500 men, and centuries, of about 80 men – even though centuries means 'hundreds'. Each legion was led into battle by soldiers carrying standards. These were decorated poles that represented the honour and bravery of the legion.

The first Roman soldiers were called up from the wealthier families in times of war. These conscripts had to supply their own weapons. In later years, the Roman army became paid professionals, with legionaries recruited from all citizens. During the period of the Empire, many foreign troops also fought for Rome as auxiliary soldiers.

Army life was tough and discipline was severe. After a long march carrying heavy kits, tents, tools and weapons, the weary soldiers would have to dig camp defences. A sentry who deserted his post would be beaten to death.

AT WAR
Trajan's Column in Rome is decorated with scenes from the Dacian wars. These were fought in the region of present-day Romania. Scenes like these can tell us much about Roman soldiers, the weapons they used, their enemies and their allies.

A LEGIONARY
This bronze statue of a legionary is about 1,800 years old. He is wearing a crested parade helmet and the overlapping bronze armour of the period. Legionaries underwent strict training and were brutally disciplined. They were tough soldiers and quite a force to be reckoned with.

ON HORSEBACK
Roman foot-soldiers were backed up by mounted troops, or cavalry. They were divided into groups, of 500 to 1,000, called *alae*. The cavalry were amongst the highest paid of Roman soldiers.

RAISING THE STANDARD

The Emperor Constantine addresses his troops, probably congratulating them on a victory. They are carrying standards, emblems of each legion. Standards were decorated with gold eagles, hands, wreaths and banners called *vexilla*. They were symbols of the honour and bravery of the legion and had to be protected at all costs.

A ROMAN FORT

The Roman army built forts of wood or stone all over the Empire. This fort is in southern Britain. It was built to defend the coast against attacks by Saxon raiders from northern Europe. Today, its surrounding area is called Porchester. The name comes from a combination of the word port and *caster*, the Latin word for fort.

HADRIAN'S WALL

This is part of Hadrian's Wall, which marks the most northerly border of the Roman Empire. It stretches for 120km across northern England, almost from coast to coast. It was built as a defensive barrier between AD122 and 128, at the command of the Emperor Hadrian.

Equipped to Kill

ROMAN SOLDIERS were renowned for their effective weapons. A legionary carried a dagger called a *pugio*, a short iron sword called a *gladius*, which was used for stabbing and slashing, and a javelin, or *pilum*. In the early days of the Empire, a foot-soldier's armour was a mail shirt, worn over a short, thick tunic. Officers wore a cuirass, a bronze casing that protected the chest and back, and crests on their helmets to show their rank. By about AD35, the mail shirt was being replaced by plate armour, in which iron sections were joined by hooks or leather straps. Early shields were oval, and later ones were oblong with curved edges. They were made of layers of wood glued together, covered in leather and linen. A metal boss, or cover, over the central handle could be used to hit an enemy who got too close.

ROMAN SOLDIERS
Artists over the ages have been inspired by the battles of the Roman legions. They imagined how fully armed Roman soldiers might have looked. This picture shows a young officer giving orders.

HEAD GEAR
Roman helmets were designed to protect the sides of the head and the neck. This cavalry helmet is made of bronze and iron. It would have been worn by an auxiliary, a foreign soldier fighting for Rome, sometime after AD43. Officers wore crests on their helmets, so that their men could see them during battle.

ROMAN ARMOUR

You will need: tape measure, A1-size sheets of silver card (one or two, depending on how big you are), scissors, pencil, pva glue, paintbrush, 2m length of cord, compass.

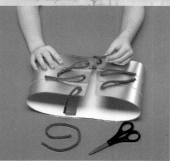

1 Measure yourself around your chest. Cut out three strips of card, 5cm wide and long enough to go round you. Cut out some thinner strips to stick these three together.

2 Lay the wide strips flat and glue them together with the thin strips, as shown above. The Romans would have used leather straps to hold the wide metal pieces together.

3 When the glue is dry, bend the ends together, silver side out. Make a hole in the end of each strip and thread the cord through, as shown above.

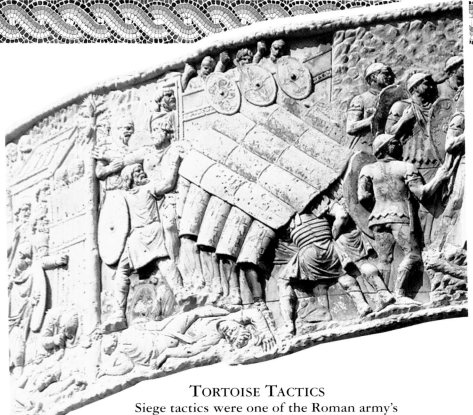

DEADLY WEAPONS

These iron spearheads were found on the site of an old Roman fort near Bath, in Britain. The wooden shafts they were on rotted long ago. Roman soldiers carried both light and heavy spears. The lighter ones were used for throwing, and the heavier ones were for thrusting at close range.

TORTOISE TACTICS

Siege tactics were one of the Roman army's great strengths. When approaching an enemy fortress, a group of soldiers could lock their shields together over their heads and crouch under them. Protected by their shields, they could safely advance toward the enemy. This was known as the *testudo* (tortoise), formation. During a siege, iron bolts and large stones were hurled over fortress walls by giant catapults.

SWORDS

Both short and long swords were kept in scabbards. This spectacular scabbard was owned by an officer who served the Emperor Tiberius. It may have been given to him by the emperor himself. It is elaborately decorated in gold and silver.

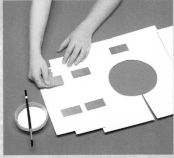

4 Cut a square of card as wide as your shoulders. Use the compass to draw a 12cm diameter circle in the centre. Cut the square in half and cut away the half circles.

5 Use smaller strips of card to glue the shoulder halves together, leaving a neck hole. Cut out four more strips, two a little shorter than the others. Attach them in the same way.

Put the shoulder piece over your head and tie the chest section round yourself. Now you are a legionary ready to do battle with the enemies of Rome. Metal strip armour was invented during the reign of the Emperor Tiberius, AD14-37. Originally, the various parts were hinged and were joined together either by hooks or by buckles and straps.

Celts Versus Romans

THE ROMANS HAD TO DO some hard fighting to win over new lands for their empire. The Celts were among their fiercest foes. There were Celtic tribes scattered throughout central and northern Europe. They shared similar languages and customs – and resistance against Roman rule! The first major conflicts began soon after 400BC, when migrating bands of Celts from France arrived in northern Italy. Then, in 387BC, Celtic warriors attacked the city of Rome itself. To the Romans, the Celts were savage, barbarian and brutal, compared with their own people. However, Roman soldiers were impressed by the courage and ferocity of Celtic warriors, and the fast, two-horse chariots that the chiefs rode into battle. The Romans soon discovered that most of the Celtic troops were no match for their well-organized, disciplined way of fighting, or for their short, stabbing swords. Once ordinary Celtic warriors saw their hero chiefs dead on the battlefield, they panicked. They either hurled themselves recklessly towards the Romans, and were easily killed, or else retreated in confusion and despair.

It took many years for the Romans to conquer all the Celtic tribes, but in the end, they succeeded.

ROMANS RIDING HIGH

This tombstone was carved as a memorial to a Roman soldier named Flavinus. He served as a standard-bearer in a cavalry regiment that was sent to enforce the Roman conquest of Britain in about AD50. The carving shows his horse trampling a Celtic warrior under its hoofs. The warrior has hair stiffened with lime to make him look more fierce. Despite their courage, Celtic foot soldiers had little chance of surviving a Roman cavalry charge.

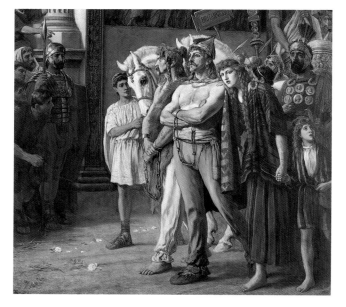

CAPTIVE CELTS
Once captured by the Romans, Celtic men, women and children were either killed or sold as slaves. This painting dates from the 1800s and shows captive Celts in Rome. The artist has invented some details of the Celts' clothes and hairstyles. After success in war, the Romans paraded captured prisoners through the city.

TRIUMPH AND DEFEAT

Two Celts, captured and in chains, are depicted on a Roman triumphal arch. The arch was built around AD25 in southern France. It commemorates a Roman victory against the rebellious Gauls. The sculptor has shown the Gauls as the Romans imagined them, looking wild and ragged, and dressed in shaggy fur.

ENEMIES ON COINS

The Romans chose to show a Celtic warrior in his battle chariot on this Roman coin. They admired certain aspects of the Celtic civilization and were proud to have conquered such a people.

JULIUS CAESAR

Roman army commander Julius Caesar was very ambitious. He used his success against the Celts in France to help advance his political career in Rome. In 44BC, he declared himself "Dictator (sole ruler) for Life". He wrote a book describing his campaigns against the Celts. Although it paints a hostile picture of the Celtic people, Caesar's book has become one of the most important pieces of evidence about Celtic life. This silver coin shows Julius Caesar, represented as an elephant, crushing Gaul (France).

WALLED FRONTIER

In AD122, the Roman emperor, Hadrian, gave orders for a massive wall to be built across northern England. Its purpose was to mark the border between lands ruled by Rome and lands further north in Scotland, where Celtic chiefs still had power. Roman soldiers were stationed at forts built at intervals along the wall. They kept a look out for Celtic attackers, but also met, traded with, and sometimes married, members of the local Celtic population who lived and worked close to the wall.

Celts Fight Back

THE CELTS RELIED ON THEIR STRENGTH – and their weapons – to survive in battle. Their heavy iron swords were used for cutting and slashing. They were carried in decorated scabbards made of bronze, wood or leather. Spears and javelins were lighter. They were used for stabbing at close quarters or for throwing at an enemy many metres away. Round pebbles, hurled by cloth or leather slings, could also be deadly weapons. Archaeologists have found huge stockpiles of pebbles at Celtic hill forts. Wooden clubs were used by warriors to bludgeon their enemies in battle, but were also used for hunting birds.

For protection, Celtic warriors carried a long shield, usually made of wood and leather. Normally, Celtic men wore a thigh-length tunic over baggy trousers but, in battle, they often went naked except for a torc (twisted metal ring) around the neck and a metal helmet. This nakedness was a proud display of physical strength – even the Celts' enemies admired their tall, muscular physique. The Celts believed that torcs gave magical protection. Their helmets, topped with magic crests, gave them extra height and made them look frightening.

CHAIN MAIL
The Celts sometimes used flexible chest coverings of chain mail in battle. Several burial sites have yielded actual chain mail such as that shown above, found in St Alban's, England. However, most of the time, the Celts went into battle naked.

UNDRESSED TO KILL
This gold pin is decorated with the figure of a naked Celtic warrior, armed with sword, shield and helmet. One ancient writer described a Celtic warrior's weapons: "A long sword worn on the right side, and a long shield, tall spears and a kind of javelin. Some also use bows and slings. They have a wooden war club, which is thrown by hand with a range far greater than an arrow …"

MAKE A SHIELD
You will need: felt-tip pen, card 77cm x 38cm, scissors, ruler, pair of compasses, bottle top, bradawl, leather thongs, paper fasteners, sticky tape, drink carton lid, plasticine, pva glue, paint, paintbrushes, dowling rod 75cm long.

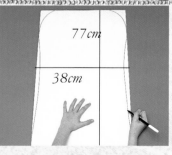

1 Draw a shield shape on to card. The shield should have rounded corners and curve in slightly on each of the long sides, as shown. Cut out.

77cm

38cm

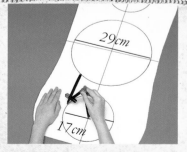

2 Draw a vertical and a horizontal line through the centre of the shield. Add a large circle in the centre and two smaller circles either side, as shown.

29cm

17cm

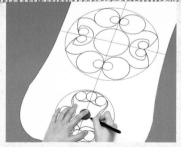

3 With a felt-tip pen draw a typical Celtic design inside the circles, as shown. Use the bottle top and compasses to help you create your design.

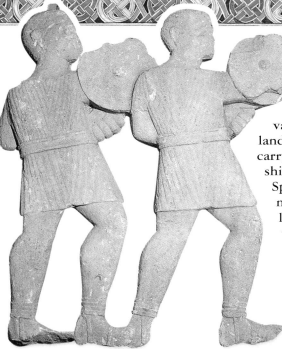

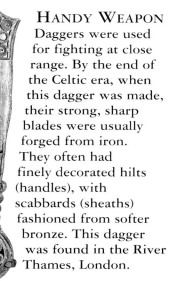

SPANISH SHIELDS

The design of weapons and armour varied in different Celtic lands. These Celts are carrying small, round shields that originated in Spain. Shields were made from wood and leather. All Spanish warriors usually fought with a short, single-edged sword, called a *falcata*.

HANDY WEAPON

Daggers were used for fighting at close range. By the end of the Celtic era, when this dagger was made, their strong, sharp blades were usually forged from iron. They often had finely decorated hilts (handles), with scabbards (sheaths) fashioned from softer bronze. This dagger was found in the River Thames, London.

BRAIN GUARD

Helmets were usually made of iron, padded inside with cloth and covered on the outside by a layer of bronze. The high, domed shape protected the wearer's skull. The peaked front kept slashing sword blows away from the eyes.

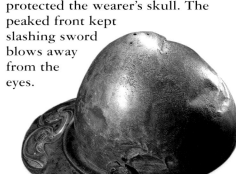

SHARP AND DEADLY

Celtic weapons were fitted with sharp metal blades, designed to cause terrible injuries. This bronze spear-point was made in Britain in about 1400BC, using techniques that were still employed by the Celts a thousand years later. Celtic metalworkers used moulds to make tools and weapons. Molten bronze was poured into the mould. Once the bronze object was cold and hard, rough edges were polished away, using coarse sand.

Shields were a speciality of craft workshops in southern England. A shield was one of a Celtic warrior's most prized possessions.

4 Use the bradawl to make two holes between the large and smaller circles, as shown. Thread the leather thongs through the holes.

5 With the bradawl, make small holes for the decorative paper fasteners. Push the paper fasteners through the holes and tape the ends on the back.

6 Stick the drink carton lid into the centre of the large circle. Roll long, thin plasticine snakes. Glue them along the lines of your decorative pattern.

7 Paint the front of the shield bronze. When dry, turn over and stick the dowling rod down the back. Use tape to secure. Tie the leather thongs.

The Fall of the Celts

CELTIC POWER in Europe lasted for around 800 years. It started to decline because other peoples grew strong enough to make their own claims for power and land. The first and most formidable of these were the well-trained, well-equipped soldiers of the Roman Empire. They had driven Celtic settlers from northern Italy in 191BC and from Spain in 133BC. After long campaigns led by their brilliant general, Julius Caesar, the Romans finally conquered France in 51BC. They invaded southern Britain in AD43, and at first met with resistance, such as the revolt led by the Celtic queen, Boudicca. Nevertheless, by AD61, the Romans controlled southern Britain, and they ruled there until AD410. However, they never managed to conquer the whole of the British Isles. Parts of Scotland and Ireland continued under Celtic rule until about AD1100. As Roman power weakened, new groups of migrants arrived, mostly from the north, to settle in the former Celtic lands. These invaders included many peoples with strong armies and vibrant cultures of their own, such as the Visigoths, the Angles and Saxons, the Franks and the Vikings.

GREAT CONQUEROR

Julius Caesar (c.100–44BC) led the Roman armies that conquered the Celts in France. He fought and won a series of battles, known as the Gallic Wars, between 58BC and 51BC. He also hoped to conquer Britain and Germany, but a political crisis in Italy forced him to return to Rome.

ROMAN STYLE

After the Romans conquered Britain in AD43, a new, mixed civilization grew up which combined both Roman and Celtic traditions. Although some Celtic chieftains rebelled against Roman rule, others decided to co-operate with the Romans, and served as local governors. They built splendid country houses, known as villas, which were decorated in the Roman style with beautiful mosaic floors such as this one.

THE VISIGOTHS

This jewelled, golden crown was made for the Visigothic kings of Spain to give as a religious offering. The Visigoths were a people from northern Europe. Celtic lands in Spain were conquered by the Romans in 133BC, and then by the Visigoths in about AD400. Even so, many Celtic skills, such as the art of fine metalworking, survived and were passed down by successive generations of settlers.

KING OF THE FRANKS

The Romans ruled France until about AD400. Northern France was then taken over by the Franks, a people from southern Germany. The Frankish kings built up a powerful empire in former Celtic France. Their most successful and powerful ruler was King Charlemagne (left), who reigned from AD771 to 814.

SAXON KING

This fine, metal helmet was made for an Anglo-Saxon warrior king. The king was buried at Sutton Hoo, on the east coast of England, the land that Boudicca once ruled. The Angles and Saxons came from southern Denmark and north-western Germany. They settled in southern England, where they established seven separate kingdoms.

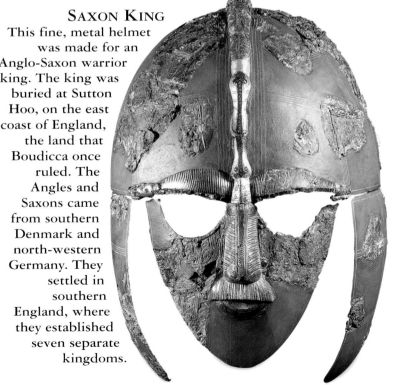

VIKING WARRIORS

The Vikings were sailors, raiders and traders who came from Scandinavia. They first attacked Britain around AD790. Soon afterwards, Viking settlers came to live in many parts of the British Isles and northern France. This tombstone shows two Viking warriors with round shields.

Viking Raids and Piracy

IN AD793, A BAND of heavily armed Vikings ran their longships ashore on Lindisfarne (an island off the north-east coast of England). It was the site of a Christian monastery. The monks tried in vain to hide their precious crosses, silver chalices and bibles, but the Vikings axed them down. They set fire to the buildings and sailed away with their loot.

BLOOD AND FIRE
This gravestone is from Lindisfarne. It shows fierce Viking warriors armed with swords and battle axes.

This was the start of the period in which the Vikings spread terror around western Europe. They began by attacking easy targets, such as villages, monasteries or other ships. They took away cattle, grain, chests of money and church bells that could be melted down. They also took women, and prisoners as slaves. Booty was shared among members of the crew. Soon the Vikings were attacking the largest and richest cities in Europe. In 846, they sacked (raided), the cities of Hamburg and Paris. King Charles the Bald of France had to pay the Viking leader Ragnar Hairy-Breeks over three tonnes of silver to leave. From 865 onwards, the English kings were also forced to pay over huge sums of money, called Danegeld. Like gangsters, the Vikings returned time after time, demanding more money – as well as land on which they could settle.

INVADING VIKINGS
This painting shows Danish Vikings invading Northumbria. The raiders soon realized how easy it was to attack neighbouring lands. They began to set up year-round war camps on the coasts. Soon they were occupying large areas of territory and building their own towns.

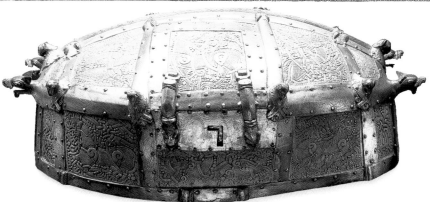

SAFE AND SOUND

Viking gold, silver and jewellery were locked in beautiful caskets and chests. This copy of a Viking chest is made of walrus ivory and gilded bronze.

ST CUTHBERT

This picture from the Middle Ages shows St Cuthbert praying in the sea. Cuthbert was one of Lindisfarne's most famous monks. He was made a saint on his death in 687. In 875, when the Danish Vikings attacked the island, the monks fled inland to safety, carrying St Cuthbert's remains.

BUILT FROM THE RUINS

In 793 the Vikings sacked the monastery on Lindisfarne, an island off the coast of northeast England. Afterwards, the religious buildings lay in ruins. The new priory pictured here was built between 1100 and 1200. The stones used to build it were taken from the ruins left by the Vikings. Today, only bare stones remain to remind visitors of the original monastery and its terrible fate.

TREASURE HOARD

Part of a Viking treasure hoard was found in a chest in Cuerdale, England. It included about 40kg of chopped-up silver, fine brooches and coins from many places that the Vikings had raided. They had sailed west to North America, south to Spain, and via European rivers to Constantinople (modern Istanbul).

The Taking of America

THE VIKINGS WERE THE first Europeans to travel to North America. Later explorers, who arrived around 500 years later, made a bigger impact. They claimed the land for their own countries and set up colonies of settlers. Commissioned by Queen Isabella of Spain, the Italian explorer Christopher Columbus landed in the Bahamas in 1492, and declared the land as Spanish territory. Spaniard Ponce de León landed in Florida in 1512, and Hernando Cortés had conquered the Aztec peoples of Central America by 1521. Tales of mountains of gold in the Southwest lured a Spanish expedition headed by Vasquez de Coronado. He encountered many native American Indian tribes, but never found gold.

The native peoples were forced from their homelands, taken captive or killed in their thousands. European explorers and colonists never regarded them as equals. They tried to force tribes to change their lifestyles and beliefs and made them adapt their traditional crafts to suit European buyers.

EARLY VISITORS
Erik the Red, the Viking king, sailed to Greenland around AD982. He was probably in search of new trading partners. His son Leif later sailed to Newfoundland and established a settlement at a place now called L'Anse aux Meadows. A trade in furs and ivory was set up with northern Europe.

SETTING SAIL
Columbus and his crew prepare to set sail from Spain in 1492 in search of a trade route to India. He never reached Asia, but landed on San Salvador in the Bahamas. The Arawaks there thought that Columbus and his men came from the sky and greeted them with praise. Columbus set about claiming the islands for the Spanish Empire. He made many of the natives slaves.

A DISTANT LAND

This map from around 1550 shows a crude European impression of North America. Henry II of France ordered Descallier, a royal cartographer, to make a map of what middle and North America looked like. The French were keen to gain land there. Jacques Cartier, a French navigator, spent eight years exploring the St Lawrence River area. He made contact with the native American Huron communities. He wrote to the king that he hoped the Indians would be "easy to tame".

MAN WITH A MISSION

A Plains Indian views a missionary with suspicion. Eastern tribes were the first to meet French missionaries whom they called "Black Robes". In California, Indians were forced to live and work in Spanish mission villages.

SAY A LITTLE PRAYER

Young Indian girls dressed in European clothes have been separated from their families and tribal customs. Europeans could not understand the North American Indians' society and religious beliefs. They wanted to convert them to Christianity, by force if necessary. In many areas, children were taken away from their people and sent to white boarding schools, given European names and taught European religion, language and history.

Aztec Power Struggles

W AR WAS ESSENTIAL to the survival of the Aztecs in Central America. They had invaded from the north from around AD1200, winning new territory by fighting the people who already lived there. From then on, the Aztecs relied on war to keep control and to win more land and cities to keep them rich. They forced the people they conquered to pay tributes of crops, treasures and other goods in return for being left in peace. The big Aztec cities such as Tenochtitlan needed steady supplies of tribute to feed their citizens. Without such riches won from war, the whole empire would have collapsed. War was also a useful source of captives, who could be sacrificed to the gods. The Aztecs sacrificed thousands of people each year, believing that this would win the gods' help.

Each new Aztec ruler traditionally began his reign with a battle. The Empire grew rapidly during the 1400s until it included most of Mexico. Conquered cities were often controlled by garrisons of Aztec soldiers and linked to the government in Tenochtitlan by large numbers of officials, such as tax collectors and scribes.

TOTONAC TRIBUTE

Ambassadors from lands conquered by the Aztecs came to Tenochtitlan to deliver the tribute demanded from their rulers. This painting shows splendidly dressed representatives of the Totonac people meeting Aztec tax collectors. The Totonacs lived on the Gulf coast of Mexico, in Veracruz. Here they are shown offering tobacco, fruit and vanilla grown on their lands. They hated and feared the Aztecs.

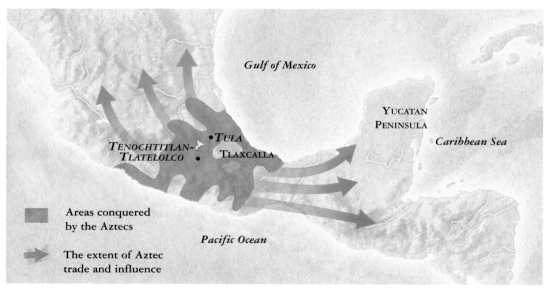

Gulf of Mexico

YUCATAN PENINSULA

Caribbean Sea

TENOCHTITLAN-
TLATELOLCO

•TULA
TLAXCALLA

Pacific Ocean

▬ Areas conquered
by the Aztecs

➤ The extent of Aztec
trade and influence

AZTEC LANDS

This map shows the area ruled by the Aztecs in 1519. Conquered cities were allowed to continue with their traditional way of life, but had to pay tribute to Aztec officials. The Aztecs also put pressure on two weaker city states, Texcoco and Tlacopan, to join with them in a Triple Alliance. One nearby city-state, Tlaxcalla, refused to make an alliance with the Aztecs and stayed fiercely independent.

CANNIBALS

One of the Aztecs' most important reasons for fighting was to capture prisoners for sacrifice. In this codex picture, we can see sacrificed bodies neatly chopped up. In some religious ceremonies, the Aztecs ate the arms and legs of sacrificed prisoners.

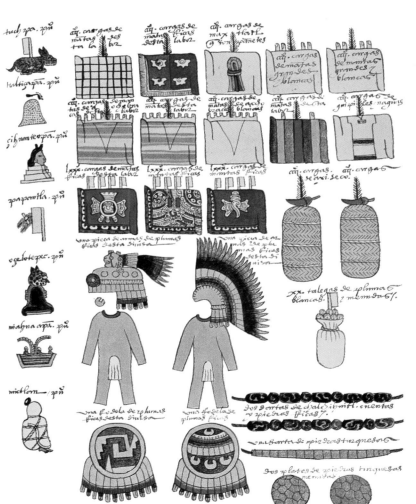

FROM HUMBLE BEGINNINGS

Aztec settlers are shown on their difficult trek through northern Mexico. The Aztecs built up their empire from humble beginnings in a short time. They first arrived in Mexico some time after AD1200. By around 1400, they had become the strongest nation in central Mesoamerica. To maintain their position, they had to be constantly ready for war. The Aztecs invented many legends to justify their success. They claimed to be descended from earlier peoples living in Mexico, and to be specially guided by the gods.

TRIBUTE LIST

The Aztecs received vast quantities of valuable goods as tribute each year. Most of the tribute was sent to their capital city of Tenochtitlan. Aztec scribes there drew up very detailed lists of tribute received, like the one on the left. Among the goods shown are shields decorated with feathers, blankets, turquoise plates, bracelets and dried chilli peppers.

End of the Aztec and Maya

I N 1493, explorer Christopher Columbus returned to Spain from his pioneering voyage to the Bahamas off the coast of Mesoamerica. He told tales of a "new world" full of gold. Excited by Columbus' stories, a group of Spanish soldiers sailed to Mexico in 1519, hoping to make their fortunes. They were led by a nobleman called Hernando Cortés. Together with the Aztecs' enemies, he led a march on the Aztec city of Tenochtitlan. For the next two years, the Aztecs fought to keep their land. They drove the Spaniards out of Tenochtitlan in May 1520, but in 1521, Cortés attacked the city again, set fire to its buildings and killed around three-quarters of the population. In 1535, Mexico became a colony, ruled by officials sent from Spain.

Similar events happened in lands controlled by the Maya people in the south of Mesoamerica, but more slowly. The Spanish landed there in 1523, but did not conquer the last independent city-state, Tayasal, until 1697.

AGAINST THE AZTECS

This picture comes from *The History of the Indies*. It was written by Diego Duran, a Spanish friar who felt sympathy for the Aztecs. Spanish soldiers and their allies from Tlaxcalla are seen fighting against the Aztecs. Although the Aztecs fought bravely, they had no chance of defeating Spanish soldiers mounted on horseback and armed with guns.

A SAD NIGHT

On 6 May 1520, Spanish soldiers massacred Aztecs gathered for a religious festival in Tenochtitlan. The citizens were outraged and attacked the Spaniards, many of whom died. During this night, the emperor Moctezuma II was stoned to death, probably by Aztecs who believed he had betrayed them. Cortés called this the *Noche Triste* (sad night).

THE END OF AZTEC POWER

This Aztec picture shows the surrender of Cuauhtemoc, the last Aztec king, to Cortés. After Moctezuma II died in 1520, the Aztecs were led by two of Moctezuma's descendants – Cuitlahuac, who ruled for only one year, and Cuauhtemoc. He was the last king and reigned until 1524.

RUNNING FOR THEIR LIVES

This illustration from a Spanish manuscript shows Aztec people fleeing from Spanish conquerors. You can see heavily laden porters carrying stocks of food and household goods across a river to safety. On the far bank, mothers and children, with a pet bird and dog, hide behind giant cactus plants.

WORKING LIKE SLAVES

Spanish settlers in Mexico took over all the Aztec and Maya fields and forced the people to work as farm labourers. They treated them cruelly, almost like slaves. This modern picture shows a Spanish overseer giving orders.

AFTER THE CONQUEST

Mexican artist Diego Rivera shows Mesoamerica after the Spanish conquest. Throughout the 1500s and 1600s, settlers from Spain arrived there. They drove out the local nobles and forced ordinary people to work for them. Spanish missionaries tried to replace local beliefs with European customs and Christianity. In Tenochtitlan, the Spaniards pulled down splendid Aztec palaces and temples to build churches and fine homes for themselves. You can see gangs of Aztec men working as labourers in the background of this picture.

Holding On to an Empire

THE INCA PEOPLE were one of many small tribes living in the Andes Mountains of Peru. In the 1200s, though, they began to take over other tribes and lands. By the 1400s, the Inca Empire covered 3,600km of the Andes and the coast. The Incas numbered only about 40,000, but they controlled a population of 12 million. They hung on to their power by military force. Borders were defended by a string of forts, and cities became walled refuges when the surrounding countryside was under attack. The permanent army of some 10,000 elite troops, could be increased substantially by those serving their *mit'a*, a system of enforced labour.

TAKE THAT!
This star may have looked pretty, but it was deadly when whirled from the leather strap. It was made of obsidian, a glassy black volcanic rock. Inca warriors also fought with spikes set in wooden clubs. Some troops favoured the *bolas*, corded weights that were also used in hunting. Slings were used for scaring birds. However, in the hands of an experienced soldier, they could bring down a hail of stones on enemies and crack their heads open.

WAITING FOR THE CHARGE
A Moche warrior goes down on one knee and brings up his shield in defence. He is bracing himself for an enemy charge. All South American armies fought on foot. The horse was not seen in Peru until the Spanish introduced it.

IN THE BARRACKS
Many towns of the Inca Empire were garrisoned by troops. These restored barrack blocks at Machu Picchu may once have housed soldiers serving out their *mit'a* (enforced labour for the State). They would have been inspected by a high-ranking general from Cuzco. During the Spanish invasion, Machu Picchu may have been a base for desperate resistance fighters.

MAKE AN INCA HELMET
You will need: scissors, cream calico fabric, ruler, balloon, pva glue, paintbrush, paints, water pot, yellow and black felt, black wool.

1 Cut the fabric into strips about 8cm x 2cm as shown in the picture. You will need enough to cover the top half of a blown-up balloon three times.

2 Blow up the balloon to the same size as your head. Glue the strips of fabric over the top half. Leave each layer to dry before adding the next.

3 When the last layer is dry, pop the balloon and carefully pull it away. Use scissors to trim round the edge of the helmet. Paint it a reddish orange.

KINGS OF THE CASTLE

The massive fortress of Sacsahuaman at Cuzco was built on a hill. One edge was formed by a cliff and the other defended by massive terraces and zigzag walls. When the Spanish invaded in the 1500s, they were awestruck by Sacsahuaman's size and defences. The Incas regarded warfare as an extension of religious ritual. Sacsahuaman was certainly used for religious ceremonies. Some historians claim that the Inca capital was laid out in the shape of a giant puma, with Sacsahuaman as its head.

SIEGE WARFARE

An Inca army takes on the enemy at Pukara, near Lake Titicaca. Most South American cities were walled and well defended. Siege warfare was common. The attackers blocked the defenders' ways of escape from the town. After the Spanish Conquest in 1536, Inca rebels under Manko Inka trapped Spanish troops in Cuzco and besieged them for over a year.

Inca helmets were round in shape and made of wood or cane. They were decorated with braids and crests.

4 Take the felt. Measure and cut a 3cm yellow square, a yellow circle with a diameter of 3cm, a 9cm yellow square and a 5.5cm black square.

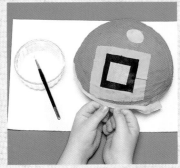

5 Glue the felt shapes on to the helmet as shown above. Glue a 2cm-wide strip of yellow felt along the edge of the helmet to neaten the edge.

6 Take 12 strands of black wool, each 30cm long. Divide them into 3 hanks of 4 strands. Knot the ends together, then plait to the end.

7 Knot the end of the finished braid. Make two more. Glue them inside the back of the helmet. Wait until it is dry before trying it on.

Spaniards Eclipse the Inca Sun

IN 1532, SPANISH SOLDIERS UNDER their commander Francisco Pizarro, landed in Peru, greedy for gold. In November, they met the Inca emperor, Ataw Wallpa, in the great square of Cajamarca. The *Sapa Inca* (Only Leader) was riding in a litter that was covered in feathers. Surrounding him, his troops glinted with gold. The sound of conch trumpets and flutes echoed around the buildings. The Spanish were amazed by the sight; the Incas looked uneasily at the strangers with their strange, fidgeting horses.

Within an hour, thousands of Incas were killed, and their emperor was in the hands of the Spanish. Ataw Wallpa offered to raise a ransom for his release, and he filled a whole room with silver and gold. Even so, in the summer of 1533, the Spanish accused Ataw Wallpa of treason, and he was garrotted (executed by strangulation). Inca resistance to the Spanish continued for another 39 years, but South American civilization had changed for ever that day.

THE WORD OF GOD?

When emperor Ataw Wallpa met the Spanish invaders in Cajamarca, he was approached by a Christian priest called Vincente de Valverde. The priest raised a Bible and said that it contained the words of God. Ataw Wallpa grabbed the book and listened to it. No words came out, so he hurled it to the ground. The Spanish were enraged, and the invasion began.

CONQUEST AND SLAVERY

The Incas were fierce fighters, but they stood no chance against the guns and steel of the Spanish. Their defeat was a disaster for all the native peoples of the Americas. Many were murdered, enslaved or worked to death in the mines. The Spanish became wealthy at the expense of the native peoples.

"SANTIAGO!"

Before the 1532 meeting with Ataw Wallpa in the great square of Cajamarca, the Spanish invader Francisco Pizarro had hidden troops behind buildings. When he shouted the pre-arranged signal of *"Santiago!"* (St James), they began to shoot into the crowd. Chaos broke out as the emperor was seized and taken prisoner.

TEARS OF THE MOON

In 1545, the Spanish discovered silver at Potosí in the Bolivian Andes and began to dig mines. The wealth was incredible, but the working conditions were terrible. Local people were forced to work as slaves. Mule trains carried the silver northwards to Colombian ports, making Spain the richest country in the world.

DESCENDANTS OF THE EMPIRE

Christians of native Andean and mixed descent take part in a procession through the city of Cuzco. In the Andes, over the past few hundred years, many Inca traditions, festivals and pilgrimages have become mixed up with Christian ones. Indigenous peoples today make up 45 per cent of the total population in Peru, 55 per cent in Bolivia and 25 per cent in Ecuador.

THE TREASURE FLEETS

The Spanish plundered the treasure of the Incas and the minerals of the Andes. Big sailing ships called galleons carried the gold and silver back to Europe from ports in Central and South America. The region was known as the Spanish Main. Rival European ships, many of them pirates from England, France and the Netherlands, began to prey on the Spanish fleets. This led to long years of piracy on the seas. Between 1820 and 1824, Spain's South American colonies finally broke away from European rule to become independent countries, but most of the region's native peoples remained poor and powerless.

Invasion of North America

ROM 1500, NORTH AMERICA was visited by the English, French and Spanish in increasing numbers. Each country laid claim to land and established colonies of settlers. It was mainly the British and the French who stayed. The first settlements were on the east coast and in eastern Canada, but gradually spread farther inland, encountering more and more tribes of native American Indians. The Europeans introduced diseases previously unknown to the Indians. A smallpox epidemic of 1837 almost wiped out the Mandan people. Fewer than 200 people survived from a tribe that had once numbered over 2,500.

From the 1760s to 1780s, colonists fought for independence from their parent countries, and in 1783, the United States became a country in its own right, independent from Britain. It doubled in size in 1803, when Louisiana Territory was bought from France for $15 million. This marked the end of French rule, and native tribes from the east could be moved west of the Mississippi River. As frontiers edged farther and farther west, more native tribes were pushed out of their homelands,

LEADING THE WAY
Sacawagea, a Shoshoni girl, guides US captains Meriwether Lewis and William Clark from Mississippi to the Pacific coast, in 1804. The journey took nearly a year. President Thomas Jefferson asked them to map out the land from the Mississippi River to the Rockies. This helped to pave the way for settlers to move to the far West.

ROLLING ACROSS THE PLAINS
From around 1850, wagon trains were signs that times were changing for the Plains tribes. Although settlers had been living in North America for around 300 years, they had mostly remained on the east coast. The US government encouraged white families to move inland.

SOD HOUSE
This is a fine example of a soddy, a house literally made from sod, or turf, cut out of the ground. Settlers had to build homes from whatever material was to hand. Life was hard for the children, they had to do chores, such as feeding chickens. If they were lucky, they went to school.

NEW TOWN

Plains Indians watch a train steaming into a new town. Land was sacred to the tribes who called it their Earth Mother. The settlers thought that the tribes wasted their land and wanted to build towns and railways on it. At first the federal government just took land for settlers. Later, they bought millions of acres of Indian land in various treaties (agreements), using force if the Indians did not agree.

PANNING FOR GOLD

A man is sifting through sand in search of gold. When gold was discovered in late 1848 in California, it started the Gold Rush. Thousands of immigrants came to the west coast from all over the world. The sheer numbers forced the tribes off their land.

TRAIN ATTACK

Plains warriors attack a train crossing their hunting grounds. The Plains tribes had always been fiercely defensive of their territory. Now they turned on the new invaders. More and more settlers were encouraged to move on to the Plains. In the 1860s, railways were constructed across Indian lands. They were built over sacred sites and destroyed buffalo hunting grounds which were essential to the tribes' livelihood. Attacks on settlers, trains and white trading posts became more frequent.

Native Americans Fight Back

WILD WEST
There were many conflicts between US soldiers and different tribes, such as this attack in the 1800s. Some attempts at peaceful talks were made. However, military records show that between 1863 and 1891, there were 1,065 fights.

W HEN THE EUROPEAN SETTLERS in North America began to fight for independence from their home countries from 1775 to 1783, some native tribes remained neutral, others took sides. Tribes who had banded together in the Iroquois League of Nations did not want to be involved in a white man's quarrel at first. They had, however, allied with the British against the French in other European wars. The League was split and eventually most of the tribes supported the British. In 1777, they ended up fighting some of their own people, the Oneidas.

Once independence had been won, the United States Government could make its own laws. In 1830, it introduced the Indian Removal Act and relocated tribes from their homelands to areas set aside for Indians called reservations. The Choctaws were relocated in 1830 to Oklahoma. They were followed by the Chickasaws, Creeks and Seminoles. Bitter battles were fought as the Indians struggled to keep their homelands. Reservation land was often less fertile and productive than the old tribal land, and some tribes faced starvation.

TRAIL OF TEARS
The heartbroken Cherokee nation is being forced to leave its homelands in 1838-39. During the trek west, rain and snow fell and soldiers made the Indians move on too quickly. It is estimated that almost 4,000 Cherokees died from exhaustion and exposure.

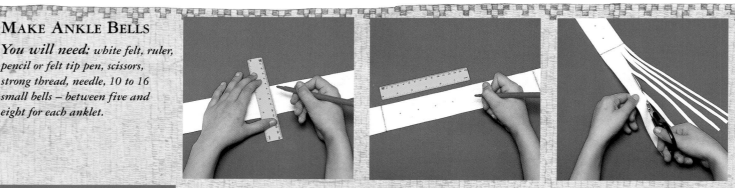

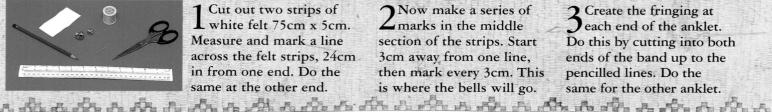

MAKE ANKLE BELLS
You will need: white felt, ruler, pencil or felt tip pen, scissors, strong thread, needle, 10 to 16 small bells — between five and eight for each anklet.

1 Cut out two strips of white felt 75cm x 5cm. Measure and mark a line across the felt strips, 24cm in from one end. Do the same at the other end.

2 Now make a series of marks in the middle section of the strips. Start 3cm away from one line, then mark every 3cm. This is where the bells will go.

3 Create the fringing at each end of the anklet. Do this by cutting into both ends of the band up to the pencilled lines. Do the same for the other anklet.

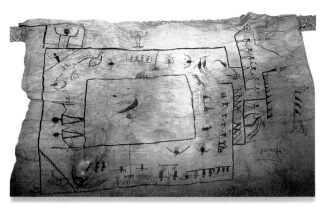

WAR BUNDLE
This buckskin was used to wrap a personal war bundle. It has been painted with the Thunderbird and other supernatural beings for spiritual protection. A bundle might carry a warrior's medicine herbs or warpaint.

THE SHIELD SURVIVED
This warrior's shield belonged to a Dakota (Sioux) warrior in the late 1800s. It may have been used in the Battle of Little Bighorn. The Sioux tribes fought in many battles with the US around that time. In 1851 their lands were defined by a treaty. Then, when gold was found in Montana, gold hunters broke the treaties by travelling through Sioux land, and war raged again.

THE END OF GENERAL CUSTER
The Battle of Little Bighorn, in 1876, is counted as the last major victory of the North American Indian. Custer and his entire 7th Cavalry were defeated by Sioux sub-tribes, after they attacked an Indian village. Sadly, this made US soldiers even more brutal in their dealings with tribes.

WAR DANCE
Sioux warriors are performing a war dance. During the dance a medicine man would chant and ask for spiritual guidance and protection for warriors going into battle. Other dances were performed after a battle.

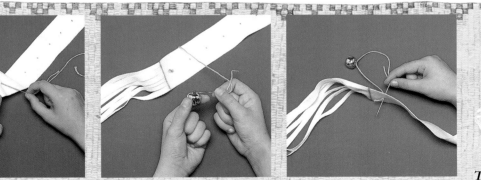
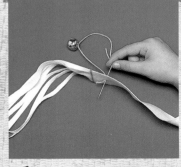

4 Thread a large needle with strong, doubled and knotted thread. Insert the needle into the fabric and pull through until the knot hits the fabric.

5 Thread the needle through the bell and slip the bell up to the felt. Then insert the needle back into the felt very near to the place it came out.

6 Push the needle through and pull tight. Knot the end (opposite side to the bell) to secure and cut away the excess thread. Repeat with the other bells.

The bells of the North American Indians were sewn on to strips of animal skins. They were tied around the ankles or just under the knees, for ceremonial dances.

Glossary

A

adobe Sun-dried mud bricks used as a building material.

alloy A mixture of metals melted together to create a new substance.

Anno Domini (AD) A system used to calculate dates after the supposed year of Christ's birth. Anno Domini dates in this book are prefixed AD up to the year 1000 (e.g. AD521). After 1000 no prefixes are used (e.g. 1429)

archaeologist Someone who studies ancient ruins and artefacts to learn about the past.

auxiliaries Soldiers recruited from non-Roman citizens.

B

barbarians Wild, rough and uncivilized people. The word was invented in ancient Greece to describe people who spoke a foreign language and whose lifestyle was different to their own.

barter The exchange of goods, one for the other.

Before Christ (BC) A system used to calculate dates before the supposed year of Christ's birth. Dates are calculated in reverse (e.g. 200BC is longer ago than 1BC). The letters BC follow the date (e.g. 455BC).

bellows A mechanism for pumping air into a fire or furnace.

bronze A metal alloy, made by mixing copper with tin.

C

catapult A large wooden structure used during a siege to fire stones and iron bolts at the enemy.

cavalry Soldiers on horseback.

century A unit of the Roman army, numbering from 80 to 100 soldiers.

chainmail Small rings of metal that are linked together to form a fine mesh, which is used to protect the body during battle.

city-state A city that with its surrounding territory forms an independent state.

civil servant Official who carries out government administration.

civilization A society that makes advances in arts, sciences, law, technology and government.

cohort A division of the Roman army, at times numbering about 500 soldiers.

colonies Communities or groups of people who settle in another land, but still keep links with their own country.

conscript Someone who is called up by the government to serve in the army.

coracle A small boat made of leather stretched over a wooden frame.

crossbow A mechanical bow that fires small arrows called bolts.

cuirass Armour that protects the upper part of the body.

currency Form of exchange for goods such as money.

D

dialects Regional accents in speech and language variations.

dictator A ruler with complete and unrestricted power.

die A tool for punching a design into metal.

dugout canoe A canoe made by hollowing out a tree trunk.

dynasty A royal family, or the period it remains in power.

E

electrum A mixture of gold and silver, used for making coins.

emperor The ruler of an empire.

empire A group of lands ruled or governed by a single country.

F

feud A long-standing quarrel, especially between two families.

frontier A boundary between two countries.

G

galley A warship powered by oars.

garrison A band of soldiers living in a particular place.

gladiator A professional fighter, a slave or a criminal who fought to the death for entertainment in the Roman empire.

greaves Armour for the legs.

H

haft The handle of an axe.

harpoon A spear-like weapon used for fishing. It has a detachable head that is tied to a line.

hilt The handle of a sword.

hunter-gatherer A person who hunts wild animals and gathers plants for food.

I

immigrants People who come to live in a land from other countries.

imperial Relating to the rule of an emperor or empress.

indigenous Native or originating from a country.
Inuit The native people of the North American arctic and regions of Greenland, Alaska and Canada.
irrigate To bring water to dry land.

J

javelin A throwing spear.
junk A traditional Chinese sailing ship with square sails.

K

keel The long beam that supports the frame of a wooden ship, running along the base of the hull.

L

latitude Imaginary lines that run parallel to the Equator of the Earth. Navigators calculate latitude to know how far north or south they are.
legion A section of the Roman Army made up of only Roman citizens.
legislation Making laws.
longitude A series of imaginary circles that pass around the Earth through the North and South poles. These are measured in degrees east and west of the Greenwich meridian. Navigtors use longitude to know how far east or west they are.

M

mercenary A soldier who fights in an army for money, not because it is the army of his own country.
merchant A person who buys and sells goods for a profit.

migration The movement of people, to other regions either permanently or at specific times of the year.
missionary A member of a religious organization who carries out charitable work and religious teaching.

N

nation Group of people who live in one territory and usually share the same language or history.
nomadic People who move from one area to another to find food, better land or to follow herds.

P

pack ice Floating sea ice.
phalanx A solid block of Greek hoplites (foot soldiers) in battle.
plate-armour Protective clothing made of overlapping plates of metal.
plunder Stolen goods.
prehistoric Belonging to the time before written records were made.
prospector A person who searches for valuable minerals such as gold.
prow The front end of a ship. Longship prows were often carved with dragon heads.

R

rampart A defensive mound of earth.
regent Someone who rules a country on behalf of another person.
republic A country that is not ruled by a king, queen or emperor but by representatives elected by citizens.
rigging The ropes used to support a ship's mast and sails.

S

scabbard The container for a sword-blade. It is usually fixed to a belt.
shield boss The metal plate that is fixed to the centre of a shield in order to protect the hand of the person holding the shield.
Silk Road The ancient trading route between China and Europe. This was the route by which Chinese silk reached Europe.
spear-thrower A tool that acted as an extension of the arm, to give an extra leverage for throwing spears.
standard A banner used by armies to rally their troops in battle or carry in parades.
stern The rear end of a ship.
surcoat A long, loose tunic worn over armour in Japan.

T

tachi The long sword that was carried by a samurai.
temple A building used for worship or rituals. Such buildings were often specially designed for this purpose.
trading post General store where people from a wide area traded or swapped goods.
treaty Peace agreement.
tribe Group of people who share a common language and way of life.

U

umiak An Arctic rowing boat made from whalebone, covered with walrus hide and waterproofed with seal oil. A umiak had a single sail and was used by the Inuit people to hunt whales.

Index

ARCTIC LANDS

ARCTIC LANDS

VIKING LANDS

North
Sea

North
America

CELTIC
LANDS

AZTEC & MAYA
EMPIRES

Gulf of
Mexico

Atlantic Ocean

Caribbean
Sea

Central
America
(Mesoamerica)

Pacific Ocean

INCA
EMPIRE

South
America

Cape Horn